How to get your
enterprise c

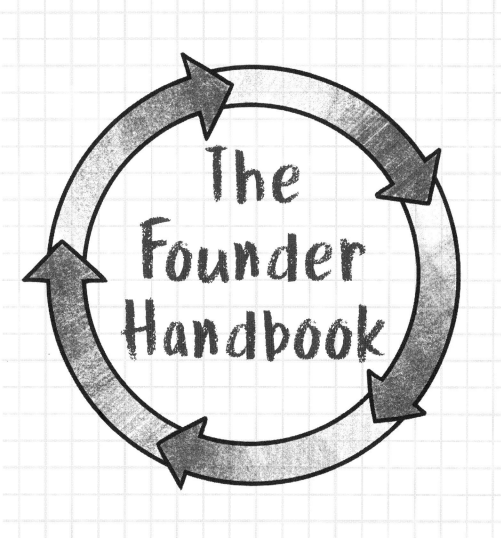

The Founder Handbook

Andrius Sutas • Siobhan Clarke

Image credits:
Page 71 (How to think about a minimum viable product): adapted
from https://linkedin.com/pulse/mvp-bike-car-fred-voorhorst/
by Fred Voorhorst; Page 189 (Your plan versus reality): adapted from
'Plans' at www.thedoghousediaries.com
To request further permissions, contact the authors at
info@thefounderhandbook.org.

Print ISBN: 978-1-838-36570-7
eBook ISBN: 978-1-838-36571-4
Audiobook ISBN: 978-1-8383-6572-1

First paperback edition January 2021.

Edited by Shari Last
Illustrations by Guy Harvey
Cover design by Plum Jam
Page design by Plum Jam

https://TheFounderHandbook.org/

About the authors

The Founder Handbook is a collection of topics from two operators: Andrius Sutas, a company founder and CEO, and Siobhan Clarke, who invests in and supports multiple startups with helping to define and execute their growth plans.

Andrius Sutas is one of the founders and CEO of AimBrain, a behavioural biometrics fraud protection company, acquired by the market leader the space at that time. Andrius and Alesis Novik founded AimBrain straight out of university as part of Entrepreneur First, a talent investment programme. Over the years, Andrius tried many approaches to starting and scaling a startup that didn't work and, with Siobhan's help, a few that did.

Siobhan Clarke is an operating partner at BP Launchpad, investing in and scaling energy companies. Previously an investor at early-stage UK fund Episode 1 Ventures, with past sales and strategy roles at Cisco, she's worked at the commercial end of technology for years. Her expertise lies in finding the value exchange and getting the right things done to accelerate early-stage companies. The techniques outlined in this book are based on Siobhan's experience of deploying and experimenting with multiple tools and frameworks at Cisco in London, Singapore and San Francisco, with Episode 1 portfolio companies and with multiple other startups.

Andrius and Siobhan worked together at AimBrain and hope to find more opportunities to work together in the future.

A note from the authors

AimBrain was a success – we worked with top-tier cloud providers and some of the world's largest financial institutions as their clients. But AimBrain was not a huge success nor a 'unicorn'.[1] Why? Because we needed to learn the lessons that we share in this book the hard way (i.e. by doing and failing) and that just took too long. This book is our version of a confession for our startup sins. While we cannot tell you how to build a successful company, and strongly believe that no one can, we definitely can share what we tried, how we failed and what we learned – distilling all of that experience into repeatable and measurable processes.

This entire handbook is dedicated to helping startups reach their first ten customers in the most efficient way and preparing for future scale. The reasons why we've focused on this will be revealed. Our aim is to answer the key 'how' questions, cutting out the noise and getting straight to the point. We wrote this book as something that we ourselves would like to read.

Connect with us at https://TheFounderHandbook.org or on Twitter @AndriusSutas and @sioclark.

Contents

The Founder Handbook

HOW TO GET YOUR FIRST TEN
ENTERPRISE CUSTOMERS

INTRODUCTION

Why does this book matter?

There are no set rules on how to succeed in building and then scaling your startup. However, we believe that there are universal lessons that every successful founder has to learn. This wisdom is usually accumulated the hard way – doing something, failing at it, learning from it and then repeating the cycle. On the outside, most companies and startups look polished, but the truth is, internally they are usually an absolute shitshow. During this book series, we'll share our experience.

There are a lot of books out there and advisors selling their 'expertise' on business-development topics. However, most of the advice is theoretical and from people who have never run a startup themselves. Everything we explore in this book, we've tried and refined ourselves, first-hand from 'the trenches'.

As the saying goes, 'A smart person learns from their mistakes. A wise one learns from the mistakes of others.' So here we are, sharing our mistakes and learnings to accelerate your journey.

Building and scaling anything means that we're all in sales. Therefore, deliberately engineering your go-to-market (GTM) strategy through the business-development process is as important as shipping an incredible product.

Sometimes, we believe that the amazing product we have created is faster, better, cheaper – and returns a massive amount of karmic goodness to the universe to boot. All you need to do is put it on your website, launch an email campaign, hire a sales team and voilà: cash flow positive by the holidays! Result!

If only it were so easy; if only people were smart enough to beat a path to your door. In reality, the whole process of thinking through what your offer is, how it is different from competing ideas, what the best ways to reach the target customer are, which use-cases to address, and how to price it… well, that's a bunch of really hard stuff that you will be constantly revising and updating as your company grows – and you need to take it as seriously as the product development itself. There is a reason why most large tech companies have enormous sales and marketing operations.

We made this mistake at AimBrain and we see it everywhere: too many early-stage companies hire the wrong sales teams too early. You bring in senior skills before really figuring out who the customer is, what you are going to sell to them and how your customer even wants to buy it.

This leads to frustration all round. Sales teams tend to be coin operated – you give them a target and they will move the company to try and reach it. This can lead to wasting engineering time, trashing pricing plans, inventing new use-cases on the fly and generally using up a lot of energy and goodwill. A properly developed and considered GTM can address all of that – but you need to take the time to do it.

Effectively, a good GTM strategy addresses the use of resources to get the product and/or service out into the market – and into the hands of customers. It sounds so simple, yet it is anything but. Common mistakes often sound like:

'It's just sales – we'll hire an awesome sales person and they'll figure it out.'

'We'll simply use the channel – we don't need a big sales team.'

'Our customers will come to us – we have a great product – they'll just find us.'

'We already talked to customers while we developed the product. It'll be fine.'

'We'll advertise on Facebook and that will work.'

'What's GTM? What's Google got to do with it?'

Death (and reincarnation) of a salesman

'The only thing you've got in this world is what you can sell.'

It's one of the most famous lines in Arthur Miller's classic play, *Death of a Salesman*,[2] and it has a certain compelling logic to it. There is a fundamentally transactional basis to any business: a customer buys something from a vendor.

Only, the concept of 'sales' has come a long way from the stereotypical heyday of the 1940s and '50s when salesmen like Miller's Willy Loman got by on their wits and would do anything to make the sale.

When it comes to the kind of companies VCs invest in today – early stage startups building the next generation of products – it is anything but the aggressive, adversarial approach of Willy Loman: vendor and customer are actually part of a single process built around shared goals. But before we look forward, let's have a quick recap.

Once upon a time, the relationship between buyer and seller was immediate and direct, based around an exchange of goods or services in return for something – bartered goods and, later, money. The seller was the maker, craftsman or grower, and so sales was not a job in its own right.

Sales as we think of it today has its genesis in the industrial revolution and the first large-scale markets that resulted from mass-produced products. It meant makers couldn't have a direct, one-to-one relationship with their customers any longer. Selling things became a profession.

Until recently, a customer was very much being sold to. They had almost no means of researching products and markets, and had to rely on the salesman to inform their buying decision. The rise of mass media, especially radio and television, presented new channels for marketing and also led to a better-informed consumer.

Sales strategies and techniques were devised, leveraging human psychology and behavioural insight in pursuit of the 'win'.

The *Mad Men* era saw things become a bit less adversarial, as salespeople started trying to identify their customers' problems and offer solutions rather than just flogging them something regardless.

As technology disrupted just about everything,[3] sales was turned inside out. The internet empowered customers with instant information about products, markets and reputations at their fingertips.

Large-scale enterprise IT sales were followed by the SaaS explosion, but even that hype curve won't be the end of the sales evolution.

So where are we now?

In a world of Artificial Intelligence (AI) and blockchain 'miracles' there is no shortage of what can look suspiciously like deep-tech snake oil. But we are also seeing truly game-changing technology find swift mainstream adoption.

As Arthur C. Clarke famously stated, 'Any sufficiently advanced technology is indistinguishable from magic'.[4] So 'selling' a piece of breakthrough product involves something like a compression of the full sweep of the history of sales, taking a pinch from each era to arrive at the close customer alignment that helps shape both product and business model.

Sure, you'll need a bit of chutzpah to get those first conversations started. A little foot-in-the-door persistence to nudge an open-ended 'maybe' into a more solid 'yes'.

But, ultimately, the sales journey is one taken by customer and vendor together and involves shared knowledge and a bespoke approach. In the case of genuinely breakthrough technology, this can take longer than typical startup cycles.

Very often, there is a pre-revenue phase of a company's development in which they are working closely with their customers to solve real business problems and achieve product-market fit. There is real value here, with a clear commitment from the customer and a honing of the product.

A startup's need to convert such initial traction into sustained growth has seen the rise of the Chief Revenue Officer. Usually, by the time a company reaches a Series A round, it will need evidence of solid sales being firmly within reach.

If the customer relationship doesn't convert into bankable revenue, generally within the first three years, it's game over – no business.

It's tempting to conclude that the old saying 'nothing happens until someone sells something' still holds true. But considering the way vendor and customer are so inextricably linked in the pre-revenue development process, it might be fairer to say that 'nothing happens until someone buys something'.

Help is at hand

Throughout this *Founder Handbook*, you'll become well versed in the details and intricacies of building a solid GTM by working directly with customers (specifically – you guessed it – your first ten enterprise customers). GTM is a foundational part of any company's strategy and is essentially attempting to answer a series of related questions through a deliberately engineered process: which use-cases, which customers, how much should we charge, what value do we bring, what demand- generation techniques should we use, what should the sales process look like, which groups within the customers should we be targeting, and how do we support them after they've committed? We outline the business-development process in ACT I.

On the route to success, there are a bunch of traps that will get you if you skip over this part of the process and just feel your way. These will cost you in terms of cash and time… neither of which you have much of as a founder.

The first trap is assumptive bias – believing what you already (think you) know about the market, your product and your own insights to create a GTM that is logical and well-suited to the business, and yet ends up having limited real connection with customers that derive the greatest value. That's a game of internal flattery. The second trap is focusing too much on one specific step in the process – it could be pricing, the actual transaction, demand marketing without conversation, etc. – and in doing so, missing the integrated cycle from your customer's perspective. GTM is a holistic, external game. It's not about internal flattery. It's about getting out and meeting with customers. It's about learning their problems, as they experience them, seeing and feeling the world through their eyes, across all aspects of the lifecycle. You must find out how your customers are measured and rewarded internally, to how they understand and describe a problem, to how they find out about you, how they buy – and indeed consume – your offering, and then how the relationship and mutual success can evolve together. This is why ACT II of this *Founder Handbook* is dedicated to refining the business-development cycle, turning the flywheel faster by incorporating customer engagement into the process.

We wrote this book as a guide that you can follow during your growth journey. We are sharing frameworks that were useful to us at that specific stage and showing you potential mistakes before they happen, as well as giving advice on how to prevent them. You will find that there are lots of cross-references across the chapters. This is to make it simple to refer quickly to related topics while reading. We want this book to be really easy to access and navigate, no matter what topic you are reading at the moment because growing your startup doesn't always follow a linear route.

CHAPTER ONE
Why do startups fail?

...AND WHAT DOES BUSINESS DEVELOPMENT HAVE TO DO WITH IT?

The first lesson that we learned from the AimBrain experience is that we should focus on being *less wrong* rather than *right*. No matter how seasoned you are, no matter how many times you've done something before, no matter how much time you spent thinking about all the potential outcomes, visualising yourself as the grand master chess player – unexpected shit will happen. Likely more often than you expect, even if you try accounting for it. As Mike Tyson once said 'Everybody has a plan until they get punched in the mouth'. We are not saying that you should not plan – that would be irresponsible to your shareholders and yourself. Instead, in this book we will be making a case for *rapid* planning based on customer feedback and iteration.

Which brings us to the main question: how can we use business development to be less wrong?

Crunchbase has probably the largest startup post-mortem archive. Based on that, they distilled the top 20 reasons why startups fail.[5] A lot of them are not reasons of failure, but *outcomes* of a single, specific type of failure. For example: 'Failure to pivot' or 'Pivot gone bad' – if business development is done diligently, you can uncover bigger business opportunities much sooner in the cycle, thus leaving you, the founders, enough runway to act on that plan and adjust with new information via continuous business development. 'No financing/investor interest' – let's be honest here, investors, just like all of us, are greedy and would not pass up an opportunity to increase their and their fund's limited partners' wealth. What they *would* pass up on is a team with no clear metrics or execution plan, making it too risky to invest. If you have done your business development diligently, you will be able to defend your case; 'Failed geographical expansion' or 'Product mistimed' – business development should be applied to all new markets, channels, customer segments, etc. This will also inform you if the market is ready and will save you and your shareholders a lot of energy; 'Lose focus' – business development distills key performance metrics that matter to the customer and informs your focus; 'Poor marketing' – business development helps to define buying personas and how to best reach them, i.e. messaging and marketing channels; 'Ignore customers', 'Product without a business model', 'User unfriendly product', 'Pricing and cost issues' or 'No market need' – you get the gist. These are all failure types that should have been addressed by the business-development process from the start.

As you can see, most startups fail because of poor business development, which *manifests* as the outcomes above.

CHAPTER TWO
What is business development?

...AND HOW NOT TO LOSE YOURSELF IN A VACUUM

The second lesson that we learned from the AimBrain experience is that you must not build a company in a *customer* vacuum – no matter what you build, how good it is or what revolutionary, cutting edge, deep-learning technique you're using, if you're not addressing real customer problems (with the right message, product, market, channel, implementation, process, value proposition, etc), your startup is extremely likely to fail. Business development is exactly that – a repeatable process that helps you to understand your customers.

Business development is a fundamental part of the company process. That's where everything starts. We can represent a business as a cycle by using a flywheel:

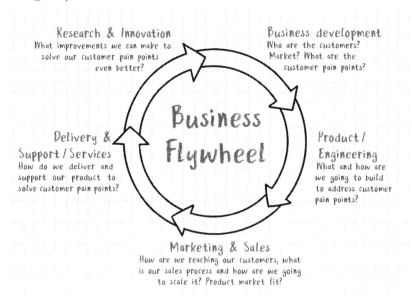

The Business flywheel. It is a fundamental, cyclical part of the company process. Each step informs the next one. It takes a huge amount of energy to start the 'flywheel' – less to accelerate and even more so to maintain.

Each step takes input from the previous one and amplifies it as an output for the following step. As Newton's First Law of Motion states '…an object in motion stays in motion…'. It is extremely important that all parts of the flywheel are accelerating together towards the same goal. If any part is malfunctioning, it causes ripple effects throughout the whole business cycle and, as a consequence, the flywheel starts slowing down. It is extremely hard to get the wheel turning initially or re-starting it after a failure. The best way to make sure it does not slow down is to understand what metrics matter at each stage of the process and measure them meticulously. As your company grows, the priorities and metrics will change, but as Peter Drucker, who is revered as the father of modern management, says 'If you can't measure it, you can't improve it'. (We discuss metrics in Chapter Nine.) In a similar way, the business-development process is also cyclical:

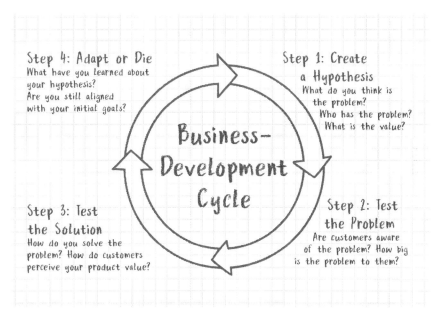

The business-development flywheel is a single step of the business flywheel, and a cyclical process that must always be done based on customer feedback. Its usefulness scales from products, which are whole companies, to single product features in a suite of offerings.

Ideas do not matter as much as the *right* execution does. With the Earth's population at more than seven billion, chances are that there are multiple people that either had, have or will have the exact same idea that you are thinking about right now. In fact, if through this process you do *not* find already existing competitors, or discover someone else who is working on exactly your problem, something is wrong. You are either in a genuinely cutting-edge academic research area, which means a PhD would be a better pursuit as it will take too long to commercialise, or others have already tried it and abandoned it – so try to understand why. Do customers actually exist for it? Is the problem real (to them) rather than perceived (as real by you)? Is the solution actually viable (within a general startup lifetime – seven years)? Is there enough value to capture? And so on. The business-development cycle is a tool that will help you to hone the *right* execution.

The reality is that getting to your first ten enterprise customers requires you to focus on business development, not on sales, not on that old startup bullshit of 'just talking to people and seeing what happens'. Focus begins with getting to the straightforward goal of ten enterprise customers very deliberately. Then, a very different activity happens after that, outside of this *Founder Handbook*, and you can tap into dozens of sales books when you get there.

What's the difference between business development and sales?
Business development is a process of discovering WHAT and WHERE. Sales is a process of taking the WHAT and WHERE and making it SCALE.

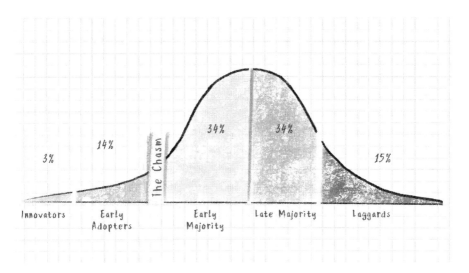

Technology adoption lifecycle and 'The Chasm'. Business development focuses on innovators and early adopters to understand what problem to solve / what to build and where the target customers are, defining a sales process where there was none. Sales, on the other hand, focuses on majority and laggards, by taking and scaling the sales process. A lot of companies fail in exactly the transition from business development to sales because they fail to adapt to the different behaviours and buying patterns of the mainstream customers.

Business development is all about finding your innovators, understanding what works and then checking your hypothesis with early adopters. Sales, on the other hand, is all about applying and adopting already-learned lessons to the early and late majorities in order to scale your business. There is a big gap between those groups, known as 'The Chasm', which Geoffrey A. Moore, a world-renowned author, speaker and advisor, goes into great detail on in his aptly named book, *Crossing the Chasm* (2014).[6] The key point to appreciate is that as you grow and scale, what you measure will change and what is success will change, so the approach to reaching different customer groups will need to change too.

Early stages are very unscalable, because they are focused on one-to-few relationships with potential customers. Yet they are the most crucial stages. They give us the insight we need to understand what the customers needs are. It is impractical to scale with this approach, but by skipping it we will not have anything to *scale*, or worse, will try to scale the *wrong* thing. Paul Graham, co-founder of Y Combinator and investor, goes into detail in one of his essays, 'Do things that don't scale'.[7] Later stages, in contrast, focus on reaching many potential customers as fast and cheaply as possible by applying the lessons learned via targeted marketing. This is the only way to truly scale.

START THE BUSINESS FLYWHEEL

The book consists of an introduction and three acts. We have already explained the importance of business development, introduced you to an overview of the usual business cycles and narrowed down the subject matter that we will focus on. Often, you can see the same ideas that we explore here expressed in different terms — we do not mind that, the important part is their execution.

ACT I is all about the basics: introducing fundamental frameworks, sharing insights and benchmarks — the tools of the trade. In other words, it is about taking the first step and setting the business flywheel in motion, while at the same time preparing a fertile ground for its acceleration, which ACT II is all about. ACT II dives a little deeper, going into the same topics but with added detail and ways to measure progress. ACT III finalises everything, as it reinforces the realisation that it is *you* who drives the company to get to the first ten enterprise customers, your decisions, with the collective insight of customers, your team and the world; you're the hero.

To some readers, ACT I might seem like the boring part — but we strongly believe that it should not be skipped — even if you already have your first customers. All of the acts build on each other and there is no magic formula for success. You need to get the fundamentals right because they will set the company's direction for years to come.

The North Star paradox

The North Star is commonly known as a single measure of core value that you deliver to your customers. It's interpreted as this one magic bullet that you find that enables success for your startup. Basically, find this North Star and the customers will line up outside your door. Wrong. The reality is that you have to work hard and consistently dig to figure out what problem you're actually solving and outline the solution and be clear on how customers are receiving value. The North Star is a combination of actions, not a single core measure and finding the North Star requires the hard work of going through the business- development cycle.

To get to ten enterprise customers, you have to get one customer first, which requires a little imagination and assumptive insight and the framework of following the cyclical process of business development:

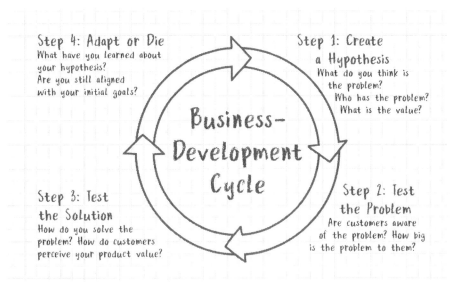

CHAPTER THREE
Step 1: Create a hypothesis

We often hear people say, 'If only I had a good idea I would start a company and be an entrepreneur'. This is delusional. What we should be asking ourselves is not 'What do I want to achieve?', but 'What am I willing to sacrifice in order to achieve my goals?'. I am yet to meet an early-stage founder (one to three years into starting a new company) that would have any sense of work-life balance. In the early days, your startup is *you*. What you can do, however, is build your life *around it*. It's important not to burn out – a startup is a marathon and not a sprint.[8] Over time, you will be able to step back, or more likely be forced to by the sheer amount of work and limited time in a day, but the early days are hard. Make sure you have a support network around you; it is extremely important and something that helped us to stay sane, as we co-founded AimBrain. Support networks can be your co-founder, other founders or a partner or spouse. However, do not expect people to empathise with you. Instead have a read of 'Here's to you, Mr. and Ms. Founder'.[9] Once you recognise what you are commiting to, how do you start? By creating a hypothesis, of course!

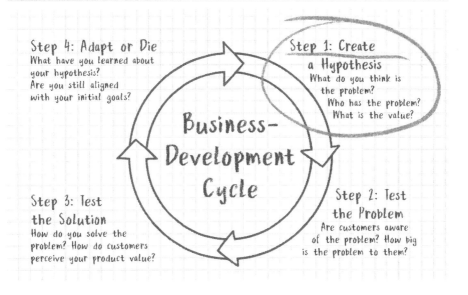

To create something from nothing we need to start with a hypothesis, a premise to be maintained or disproved. Each time you have an idea, train yourself to answer the fundamentals:

1. Who are the customers?
2. What are their problems, needs or desires?
3. How do you solve them?
4. What is the value that you create for the customer?
5. How do you reach the customer?
6. Who do you compete with (think beyond just direct competitors – what are the current solutions that you will need to displace)?
7. What are your advantages over the existing solutions?

The questions above make up the basis of the 'Lean Canvas model', and help you to get into a customer-focused mindset.

Idea generation

'Start with a hypothesis' is easier said than done. Your goal is to find problems that you yourself could solve relatively soon (for example, trying to commercialise cutting-edge academic research is rarely a viable path for a high-growth startup). Ideally, find problems where you have an unfair advantage, maybe they are problems you have yourself or that you have a unique insight into (for example, through current employment or industry knowledge). From our experience it is very hard to find problems 'on demand'. It is much easier to create a system for taking notes and giving it time. That way, once you are ready to take the leap into entrepreneurship, you will have a database of potential ventures to explore on day one.

Be careful you don't just jump on the first idea that excites you – time on this planet is limited and you should always consider the opportunity cost, the loss of other alternatives when one path is chosen. At the other extreme, do not procrastinate on looking for that 'perfect' idea –

it's just fear of execution. A good approach to exploration and decision making is the 37% rule, a mathematical approach to maximising satisfaction and minimising regret. This is known as the 'optimal stopping problem'.[10] To generalise it, spend 37% of the time (or options) you have to explore, rejecting them as a learning experience, and after that pick the immediate best option, as compared to the initial ones, from those that you see next, or the last one if there are no better ones. Set yourself a realistic timeline based on your circumstances (for example, aim to have first customers a year from now) and divide that time into 37% exploration and 63% execution. From our experience open-ended exploration never works as there is no clear decision point. This is also why internally self-imposed deadlines are as important as customer deadlines. Hint: The 37% rule applies to a lot of places in life involving choice, such as hiring, fundraising and even dating. You cannot be always right, but this way you will be less *wrong*.

Have a system where you write down all your ideas – a 'problem journal'. The goal here is to build a habit for capturing your ideas. Don't bother judging or evaluating them just yet. You can't fully control when new ideas come, but, there are activities that can stimulate them:

1. **Personal problems.** Look around and be mindful of your behaviour. What frustrates you the most? Where do you spend the most money? What takes the most of your time? What do you procrastinate most on? Why? Are there any inefficient habits that can be automated? Note those down. For example, one of the reasons we started AimBrain was that we were fundamentally dissatisfied with the way digital banking and identity works. You have to carry hard tokens and enter random digits from your password. The institution treats you as an imposter until you prove them otherwise (for example, even if *they* call you, you need to answer a security questionnaire – a broken process which in fact opens up vectors for social

engineering. There must be a better way!). Our hypothesis was that things are created *by* people *for* people and those things need to serve *us*, rather than the other way around. You are unique and you should not need to prove to *things* it is indeed you. It should just work.

2. **Primary job and area expertise.** Look for insights that give you an unfair advantage. Are there projects you are working on that imply business opportunities? For example, what tools does your company use? What are the most common complaints from your co-workers? Are there any tools that your company needs, but cannot buy and thus need to build in-house? Are there inefficient processes that could be automated by a standalone tool? What are top priorities for your company? (For example, reducing fraud, generating revenue, reducing call centre wait times.) What teams of people work there and can their function be automated?

3. **Hobbies.** Work on something completely different to your day-to-day activities. What unserved needs have you observed? What took most time to build that could be generalised? How big is your hobby community? What does the community most often complain about?

4. **Social circles.** Talk to people – the more diverse the better. What tool or service do they use most often? What do they complain about? What are their goals and motivations? Even better, shadow someone in-person in their usual work environment. On what do they spend most of their time? What makes them annoyed or non-productive? What can be improved?

5. **Forums and news sources.** Read HackerNews, Reddit or Twitter. What do people complain about? What services are they trying to solicit? Do you see your potential competitors receiving a lot of complaints – how can you solve those?

Quantity produces quality. By training your brain to note problems, it will become more efficient and that in itself will make you notice more opportunities. By repeatedly following a business-development framework, you will train yourself to be more critical and methodical with idea evaluation. Thus, constant training (quantity) improves the skill (quality).

Product versus services versus solution

These three terms are often used interchangeably, but with very different definitions:

- **Product** is a tangible item that can be consumed in some way by the customer. It has features that perform (usually automate) processes. Costs are deterministic, thus the pricing can be pre-determined and is based on usage or features. Costs scale at a lower rate than revenue. Usually requires investment upfront to then derive value later. Should always be reused with new or different customers with no or minimal changes. Usually based on engineering output.

- **Services** is an intangible item that is performed to or for the customer. It can have a standard process/approach, but it does require tailoring for each individual case. Costs cannot be determined ahead of time, only work-unit rates and, at best, an estimated effort. Costs scale linearly with the revenue. Usually has low upfront setup costs. Can rarely be re-used with new or different customers. Usually based on human capital.

- **Solution** is an *outcome* of applying a product or services to solve a customer problem. Focus is on benefits, rather than features. Pricing is based on the value created, delivered or captured, rather than costs.

Lean Canvas model

You should take each rough idea that you've come up with and look at it in a structured way, in a Lean Canvas model, which will be the first working version of the hypothesis. The goal is to keep updating your model with new insights and quantifiable information until you have validated your assumptions – or to iterate/pivot based on your target customer feedback.

Lean Canvas captures the two most important risks for an early business:

1. Market risk – is there a market for your product?
2. Product risk – can you actually build the product?

We know that the Lean Canvas has been around for a while and is well used in accelerators and early-stage advice camps. We've seen it used with disastrous outcomes, when founders have treated it like a box-ticking exercise – doing it only because investors asked them to, not really thinking through each field and hoping to 'wing it' or simply not doing it at all. DO NOT. At AimBrain, we tried to keep it only in our minds, not writing it down, at first – and learned quickly that such an approach does not scale with new learnings and makes it impossible to communicate company direction consistently. Putting thoughts in a framework helps weed out assumptions and provides a consistent direction for everyone. Only once your thoughts have been organised into a structure, can you understand what you are testing your hypothesis against.

The Lean Canvas, by Ash Maurya, takes the idea from Business Model Canvas, by Alex Osterwalder, but focuses on the customer, problem and solution.[11] It has been designed to specifically reflect the most uncertain areas of an unvalidated startup business model. By forcing your thoughts into a defined structure using the Lean Canvas, you also aid clarity for yourself in your own approach[12] and help to communicate your thoughts efficiently to any external stakeholders. Only once the idea is validated by the market (showing a product-market fit), would you switch to a traditional Business Model Canvas, which would then allow you to optimise and scale an existing process. The Lean Canvas is usually represented as follows:

Problem	Solution	Unique Value Proposition	Unfair Advantage	Customer Segments
Top 3 problems	Top 3 features	Single, clear, compelling message that states why you are different and worth buying	Can't be easily copied or bought	Target customers
	Key Metrics Key activities you measure		Channels Path to customers	

Cost Structure	Revenue Streams
Customer Acquisition Costs Distribution Costs Hosting People, etc.	Revenue Model Life Time Value Revenue Gross Margin

PRODUCT	MARKET

Less is more. The Lean Canvas is meant to capture the essence of your business, rather than an execution plan or multiple GTM strategies. If you are unable to concisely define each field by distilling it into two or three bullet points, chances are that you have not yet fully understood the area and need further insight – it may also suggest that the product or market approach is too broad and needs to be cut down.

Problem

A fundamental question: what are the top two or three customer problems? Do not worry now about getting the problem statements exactly right, however, do your research ahead of the time – it is likely that a lot of your questions can be answered with a simple web search. This will show the potential customers that you are not just wasting their time, but have put effort into understanding their field first.

Potential ideas:

- **Search for literal statements for what you are trying to learn.** For example, 'What is the cost of fraud to a company'. You will find a lot of blog posts and marketing materials that will help you to see multiple viewpoints and form an opinion of your own.
- **Search for general market reports (for example, Gartner, Forrester, Aite, etc).** Do bear in mind the dirty business secret: most of the time, reports are initiated and paid for by the company that is praised the most in it. Read a lot, but be critical of any assumptions or recommendations. Instead, look at the data and draw your own conclusions, then validate them with your target customers.
- **Search for market-specific thought leaders and reports.** This can include individuals on Twitter, specific LinkedIn groups or advisory companies and workgroups focused on a specific sector.
- **Read everything you can that is published by your potential competitors.** If the company is public, look at investor and shareholder packs. They contain a goldmine of information about near and long-term priorities, performance metrics and KPIs. As the saying goes, 'good artists copy, great artists steal'. It took a lot of energy for your competitors to be in the position they are in today – use their work as a shortcut to learning market needs, industry keywords and product metrics that customers have already been trained to recognise as the most important and differentiating.

We found that the most effective way to discover the underlying problem is to apply a root-cause analysis, or to ask 'The Five Whys'.[13] As we discussed in Chapter One, observable problems are usually a manifestation or an outcome of fundamental events or choices. By asking 'Why?' multiple times you are able to learn the causality of the system. Some events that cause problems are genuinely beyond your control (for example, political or global acts), but you need to be careful to not give in to simple answers. For example, 'I am unable to deliver this project on time because I need more people'. Chances are, the fundamental problem was at estimation and/or management level, rather than headcount. The former would lead you towards creating a project orchestration framework, whereas the latter would perhaps warrant an HR recruitment firm. Both are good, but only one can scale exponentially (hint: it's not the one that generally relies on people day-to-day, as opposed to technology, to grow).

Understanding the problem clearly will also help you find the target customer trigger words for marketing. For example, your customer wants to enable remote onboarding or digital identity verification. Why? To onboard new customers faster. Why? To offset the churn from leaving customers and to increase the user base. Why? To increase their profit margin. Why? Because competition is stealing the markets and that negatively impacts operational costs. Based on the analysis, you can safely say that new revenue and reducing operational costs are the driving factors, and thus triggers, behind the initiative. Now you can use those keywords in your customer meetings and, at the future scale, marketing campaigns.

When you answer the question correctly, you are on the path to success. But when you don't answer it correctly, you are overwhelmingly likely to fail.

Customer segments

Be as specific as possible when defining your target customer segments. We are yet to see a startup that was 'too focused' early days, but too many that went after everyone and, as a consequence, didn't meaningfully reach anyone. Generally, you want to create an individual Lean Canvas for each customer segment as other elements of the model will vary based on it. (Many different companies might have the same exact problem, but how you approach it and solve it will likely vary greatly.)

Who are your target customers? Who are *their* target customers? What's your target customer industry segment? How big are they (for example, number of employees, different industries served, online presence, etc)? Where are they geographically? What products or services do they tend to use? What are specific past observed behaviours (product releases, marketing announcements, significant company events, etc)? What is their buying frequency and average purchase size?

If your target customers are other startups – what stage or maturity have they reached? How much total funding do they have? What technology stack do they tend to use? What operational or execution risks do *they* have?

If you're working on a marketplace or your customer segments are interdependent – do you understand all involved stakeholders or market sides and their incentives equally well? How will you bootstrap one side to get the marketplace started?

Note the difference between customers and users – while the latter means someone who uses your product or service, the former is someone who pays for it. More often than not they are not the same entity.

Solution

What does a minimal solution or smallest offering (minimum viable product) that addresses your target customer problem look like? What are the top two or three features that are fundamental to your customers?

Unique value proposition

The unique value proposition, also known as the unique selling point or USP, combines the problem with your solution. A clear and quantified statement of why customers should use your product, as opposed to competitors or, in fact, as opposed to using no product at all. But remember this about your customers: changing direction or old habits is hard. It is not enough to demonstrate to the customer that they can have incrementally better performance – we need to demonstrate a tenfold change from their *current* practices, if any, and we need to demonstrate why *we* are the ones to facilitate that change. The unique value proposition will form the basis of your marketing strategy and needs to appeal to a specific buying persona.

Unfair advantage

What measurable and factual advantage do you have against your competitors *today*? It can be your geographic location (i.e. feet on the ground, enabling you to see customers in person on a short notice); expertise (e.g. prior companies or job experience in a specific field); networks (e.g. you know many target customers on a personal basis) or community that you can sell immediately into (e.g. you created a target community by working on indirect projects or positioning yourself as an expert in the field). Expect to be asked what is your advantage by investors – why they should invest in you as opposed to your competitors.

Channels

What is our path to the customer? What is their preferred buying method? Be careful not to fall into the trap of thinking that you need partners early on. We talk about how partners can be useful to scale in Chapter Seventeen. But in these early days we need to understand customer problems and therefore the most efficient way to do it is by having direct customer relationships. Be as specific as you can and skip the obvious (e.g. word of mouth

– a consequence of marketing reach and good product, rather than a channel – or search engine optimisation, which you should be doing anyway). A few examples of the best early channels:

- **Direct social media**. LinkedIn – start here. Search by specific company names, titles, geographies, etc. From our experience, LinkedIn works as good as emailing that specific person.

- **Mailing lists**. For example, from your signup page. Forums, groups and other sector-specific communities. Register and participate in discussions. Reach out to individuals if possible. Get in touch with group administrators and ask if you could be put in touch with a few target customers or if you could run a workgroup or deliver a short presentation during one of their events.

- **If you already have investors, explore their connections**. Ask for specific introductions, as well as, who they can think of reaching out to. Use them as much as you can – after all, your success is also their success.

Fundamentally, think about where your target customers hang out and learn about new industry trends. Focus there as your first channel.

Examples of later-stage channels:

- **Engineering as marketing and content marketing.**[14] Publish technical blogs covering the area you are in and how you are addressing industry-unique challenges; devise and give out branded free-of-charge tools related to your industry or product, that are relatively uncomplicated to make, but improve life quality significantly (e.g. if you are building a solar system monitoring dashboard, think about creating a calculator that would show time to recoup the initial investment for consumers or a tool that would calculate the optimum angle for solar panels based on location. Your target customers might end up using it in their own operations); write branded reports that cover the industry (e.g. an overview and proposed direction of legal or regulatory changes, customer insights, customer behaviours, unique statistics, etc). The goal here is to get your name or brand in front of potential customers using tools and resources to increase brand familiarity[15] and generate leads.

- **Affiliates**. Build sector-specific relationships with third-party brands that mostly provide value through services (e.g. generating industry reports and positioning you positively, running industry forums and sharing your brand as someone to work with or consulting services who will recommend your product directly). Affiliates are different from partners in that they usually do not have a product and do not integrate or package yours to create something new. Be mindful to not rely too much on this channel – your competitors can simply pay more and you will quickly find yourself forgotten.
- **Referrals.** Use your existing customers for these. Think how can you turn them into your brand ambassadors by rewarding them for inviting their peers. This is an important one as it creates a viral loop if executed well.
- **Events.** From our experience, trade shows generate the lowest ROI out of all marketing channels. To optimise, always try to get a keynote speaker spot. Consider if there are smaller, but highly targeted groups that you could join or even lead (e.g. local meetups). Sponsoring hackathons is fun, but at AimBrain we learned that during a hackathon, participants just do not have enough time to explore the available tools in depth. (Hint: they are, however, a great place for recruitment at a later stage.)

Be sceptical as soon as you hear another party positioning themselves as 'strategic' to you. 'Strategic alliance', 'strategic partnership' or 'strategic insert-any-word-here' usually means that it will lose you money, otherwise you would be discussing hard numbers based on their past successes with companies similar to yours in a context *mutual* value, as opposed to how 'strategic' the relationship *will* be.

Cost structure

What costs will you incur upfront and how does it look like on an ongoing basis? Quantify and minimise. Examples:

- Salaries/people/office space
- Software development/consultants/legal
- Cloud costs
- Payment network fees
- Third party vendor fees
- Marketing/group memberships
- Equipment/premises

Revenue streams

How will you generate revenue? How expensive will your service or product be, will there be pricing tiers? What will your margins be? What is a one-off, what is repeatable? If repeatable, is it a periodic subscription or an annual license – or something else?

How much you charge will change over time, according to the price discovery process which we talk about in Chapter Six. In the early days, the simpler the better.

Key metrics

What are the top two metrics that are a proxy for immediate progress and long-term success, your North Star metrics? This needs to reflect your main activities and how you measure them. As an early high-growth business your overall main goal is to capture value. But at the very beginning, you need to find product-market fit, therefore the best metrics that you can capture in the early days are around learning, for example:

- Number of business development customer interviews
- Number of signed Letters of Intent

- Cold outreach conversion rates (which will also improve as you nail down the specific problem, solution and industry language)

Over time your value definition will shift. For a B2B company, value is best represented by revenue. Consulting (professional services) and one-off revenue is OK in the early days, but you need to have a clear understanding of how that converts repeated revenue down the line. For a VC-backed venture you need to be in a position where value scales exponentially. We talk about key metrics and how to capture it in Chapter Eight.

The metrics you set will drive human behaviour. This applies to you, your team and your company board. It is important not to lie to your (potential) shareholders, and more importantly, to yourself. It is very easy to find a metric that makes you feel good and as if you are making progress, when in reality, you are wasting time and energy on vanity goals.[16] We know that we have done this multiple times. These are some examples of metrics that we had at some point at AimBrain that turned out to be a complete waste of energy:

- **Pageviews.** You hear about 'tracking pageviews' a lot. What we observed at AimBrain was that an increase in pageviews did not lead to an increase in signups. Marketing was happy and we had nice graphs going up. Our website was *seen* by more people, but not necessarily at the right time in their buying cycle. Our website had also not been well-tailored to our target persona, so it wasn't converting well enough. (It was driven by product features rather than problems and trigger keywords). Unless you receive revenue directly per pageview, we found that growing our mailing list and producing content had a much better ROI for lead generation.
- **Registered users.** So you have visitors who are converting to registered users – perfect, you might think, we fixed our funnel! Not so fast. When we focused on registered users at AimBrain,

we, again, increased that number, plotted growing graphs and patted ourselves on the back. The problem was that while people registered, our product *usage* did not actually increase. What we learned was that we tried to scale before fully understanding our target personas and how to drive their behaviour. We had wrong messaging. Furthermore, it did not help that once a lead would register for a trial they would not see immediate value in our service, and never come back – hence signups going up, but usage remaining the same. It might be obvious looking back, but make sure that you have a clear, and preferably automated, onboarding process that takes the user through absolutely the minimum amount of steps as fast as possible and provides all the tools for demonstrating your product's value, as well as, communicating *exactly* what that value is. Track *usage* and understand where your potential customers drop off and why. Your task is to get to ten enterprise customers, so ensure that clear path to conversion.

Identify exactly what metrics really matter to your growth and the success of the product. Then, learn how to measure them with as little noise as you can. Finally, be obsessed about constantly improving them.

CHAPTER FOUR
Step 2: Test the problem

I remember my very first customer conversation at AimBrain. I was scared. What if they don't like what we're working on? What if they think I am stupid? What if... my ego is hurt? My imagination could not have been further from the truth. 80% of the people we reached out to never even responded. This is in no way a failure – everyone has the same 24 hours in a day and your message needs to compete with their colleagues' needs, family emergencies and personal hobbies. Sometimes it is genuinely just bad timing and other priorities push your message down to a point where responding a month later would be just awkward. 5% of people that we reached out to got upset with us for sending them a *single* message. I remember to this day the most passive aggressive one-line response – 'Thanks, but no thanks. Never message me again'. Everyone has bad days – do *not* take it personally, and never get upset because, remember, you have no right to their time. Be thankful that now at least you know you guessed their email correctly. The remaining 15% of people that we reached out were an absolute goldmine! They were happy to talk to us, shared their personal experience from current and past ventures, industry insights, and some even connected us with someone from their own personal network that we could speak to as well. Those 15% of people are more than worth all the effort – their knowledge will be part of steering your company to success. Nowadays, I find customer conversations the most exciting part of launching something new. They are also the best use of time a founder can make.

Now is the time to look at your Lean Canvas and take the second step of the business development cycle towards testing and validating your problem hypothesis – talk to the customers through the channels you identified.

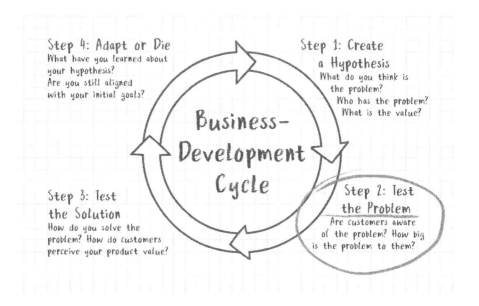

The art of good questions

Start the learning process. Before you jump to a solution you need to understand if the problem you are trying to address even exists. We have two ears and one mouth – use them in proportion. The best learning will take place when you listen to *understand*, rather than to *respond*.[17] It is a privilege when someone agrees to share their time with you[18] and you must do your homework beforehand to make the best use of it. Start with the Problem, Customer segments, Channels, Revenue streams and Unique value proposition sections of the canvas and write down fundamental questions that would help examine your core assumptions. Aim for no more than 12 questions in total (approximately five minutes each for a one-hour session) and rank them by importance – the top ones will usually be related squarely to the problem section. Always have your top three questions in your mind – you never know when you will find yourself sitting next to a potential customer in a coffee shop or at a conference. Expect to iterate on the depth and breadth of the questions as you go through the process.

Customers lie. It is extremely important to phrase questions correctly as customers will lie. It is not their fault. Most often, they do it unconsciously and, in fact, normally think they are doing you a *favour*. Rob Fitzpatrick, tech founder and author, explores why this happens and how to best approach it in his book *The Mom Test* (2013).[19] The key takeaway is that we need to ask for facts, rather than opinions:

- If the information you hear contradicts your assumptions – good, you really want that as it will enable you to iterate faster.
- Remember ego? Ignore it for now – compliments, ideas and suggestions feel good but they are distractions to your primary goal: problem validation. If you leave a meeting with loads of compliments and no contradictions or new learnings to adjust your hypothesis, it was a waste of time and a missed opportunity.
- Take a note of suggestions that are based on industry insight rather than individual preferences – it might provide a hint as to where you need to look next. There is a difference between 'I do not like to take photos of my face and therefore do not think biometrics will ever replace passwords, I suggest you sell hard tokens for authentication' and 'I suggest you look at the latest European Biometric Identity Workgroup report – they have a direct impact on regulation and their last report promotes hard tokens heavily'. Latter is significantly more useful to you.
- Be specific and always quantify: 'frequently', 'sometimes' and 'often' are not words you can work with. Your aim is to build a scalable process – imagine explaining to a computer that it should do a task 'frequently'... What does 'frequently' *actually* mean – five times an hour or five times a year? That is a difference of 8,760 times and you'd better believe that will have

a direct impact on your pricing and costs.

- The 'will', 'might' and 'would' are excuses for not doing something now. How often from your past experience, when someone said 'I *will* think about it', did they actually do it so that it progressed anywhere? How often from your past experience has someone said 'I *would* definitely buy it' and actually bought it? It almost never happens. These are social constructs meant to keep your ego intact without telling you the truth in fear of coming across as confrontational. No one likes to burn bridges. So avoid 'will', 'might' and 'would' and ask direct questions – when was the last time you did it? What prevents you from doing it today? How much do you spend on it monthly? Whatever 'it' and 'do' might be.
- Customers do not always know what they want. It is unclear if Henry Ford, founder of Ford Motor Co., actually said it, but the concept of 'If I had asked people what they wanted, they would have said faster horses.' is very relevant to customer conversations. Remember 'The Five Whys'. It is your job to increase signal-to-noise ratio, i.e. understand the underlying problems while ignoring all the fluff that is the inevitable part of social conversation.

First conversation with a potential customer

Ask for forgiveness and not for permission. Your goal is to get your problem hypothesis validated as fast as possible. Fast validation ideally gives you more time for execution and at worst – leaves you more time to pivot. Warm intros (when someone introduces you to someone new that they themselves know) will always have a higher conversion than cold outreach. We talk about the latter in the 'Follow Me Home' section. However, do not fall into the trap where you wait for an introduction while not reaching out to new potential clients yourself. Even to a different group or a person within the same organisation. We have seen too many first time founders, including ourselves, make this mistake. Excuses like 'it will come across as unorganised' or 'that intro will come through soon, so no need to do anything else' is just your fear manifesting as procrastination (which also comes in many other forms – building products or features before working on the business development, not being persistent in the process, expecting that someone else will help to solve your problems, etc). If you have already spoken to someone in an organisation that you later get introduced to, use the situation to your advantage – name drop the other party as a statement of fact at the start of the session. In an extremely unlikely event where you are talking to someone who feels that all external conversations need to go through them and they get a little bit upset that they were not the first ones you have spoken to, just explain that you are at early stages of market exploration and that it is useful to hear a perspective from someone who might not even be part of the relevant target market. Take it away from them and focus it on yourself – there are often internal politics at play that you do not want to waste your energy on.

Start in the middle. At first you might not know exactly what seniority your target customers are. Too senior – they will just ignore your outreach over other tactical priorities; too junior – they will just not have enough influence or strategic outlook. It is an iterative process and best to start somewhere in the middle, measure conversion and note learnings within the Lean Canvas. To close a sale you will usually need support from both, higher and lower seniority people within the organisation. However, your goal now is to understand the best entry point, which will define your buying personas. Think if after the first conversation you usually get introduced to more senior or more junior people? A different team or business unit? Try starting there next time.

Appeal to self-esteem. You might be wondering why anyone would take the time to talk to you. If we look at Maslow's Pyramid of Needs we will find the answer – self-esteem. A lot of people are driven by wanting to be respected. You reaching out to them as the field or industry expert appeals to that. People also like to be recognised by others. You are, by definition, building something new, so when you share the latest industry trends and hint at your own new ideas, they will be able to share the learnings with their peers and appear knowledgeable of the latest advancements. It also appeals to people's desire for freedom. A lot of nine-to-five employees have considered starting a business themselves, but it is not part of their daily job scope, hence it breaks the routine. So make your conversation a bidirectional value exchange.

Be wary of innovation teams. It is paradoxical, but enterprise innovation teams usually do not produce actual innovation. It is not their fault, but rather a consequence of how large businesses operate. On paper, the company needs to be doing 'innovation' and what is the easiest way to show that? To create a standalone innovation team. Usually the team has non-business focused KPIs, such as a number of organised 'innovation' events or a number of different startups spoken to, which is exactly where the problem is – they rarely know what the top problems are in their different internal business units. In the rare cases where they are vaguely aware of the top issues, they still don't have any control or influence over production budgets – only business units do. It is then no surprise that they bring 'innovation' which is pushed aside by other priorities. In some organisations it goes as far as to put a negative flag on any startup that comes through the innovation team, meaning that you will very likely have a significantly harder time in getting the attention of your potential decision makers, than if you had just reached out to them directly yourself.

Follow the session etiquette. Make it convenient for *them*. Do they have an office in the same city? Go see them. Do they prefer a call? Arrange conference call facilities yourself. Different time zone? Make sure it fits into *their* schedule. Set expectations ahead of time and reiterate at the start of the session that you are not here to sell, but to learn. Strictly no slides. This will make people more open in sharing and lower their defences. No one likes being sold to and, in fact, at this stage there is nothing to sell. Aim to have two people join from your side, including you. Being a single person makes it too hard to take all the notes while progressing the conversation or listening for insights and key ah-ha moments. Three is a group and could make the other person feel a little ambushed, thus less inclined to help you. Two is optimal and gives you two perspectives for your Interview Output Canvas.

Some of these business development sessions will indeed result in actual clients. We talk about follow-up actions and nurturing in the 'Follow Me Home' section. It is unlikely that you will get all your questions answered in one session – that is fine. If you have never spoken to the person before, even if it was a warm introduction, schedule your first session for one hour. This will give you a good sense of your chemistry with the person. If it is going well, thank them for their time and insights so far and ask if they can go over the allotted time. Alternatively, ask if it would be possible to touch base with them again with any clarifications. If the conversation is going nowhere, or the person feels hostile (which happens sometimes through warm introductions where the person is doing a favour to your contact, but doesn't really want to be engaged), or if there is just no chemistry, be generous in your praise of their ideas – you might meet them again in the future and make sure to leave a good impression irrespective of how you feel. Often people might not know exact answers or numbers – ask them if it would be OK to follow up on that after the meeting. Do not push too much – sometimes 'I don't remember' actually means 'I am unable to tell you due to NDAs in place (but I like you, so I do not want to come across as incompetent or hostile)'.

After each session make sure to follow up with a thank-you note and any agreed action items. This is an opportunity for you to show that you are trustworthy. Have you promised to make any introductions? Have you offered to share any additional materials? Have you mentioned any groups, articles or resources that might be of interest? Inversely, have they done any of those? If they were not the right person for exploring the problem, can they connect you with someone who is better suited?

Interview Output Canvas

You can only improve what you measure. It is important to capture the information while it is still fresh in your mind, straight after the meeting, via an Interview Output Canvas:

Conducted DD/MM/YYYY

Company: Company Name
Who: Name & title
Segment / Market Focus:

#Customers & type:
Revenue:
#Employees:
Founded in:

Discussion Summary
· Outline short points relevant to the discussion

Key Ah-has (key learnings that you didn't understand before)
· 2-4 key ah-has at most

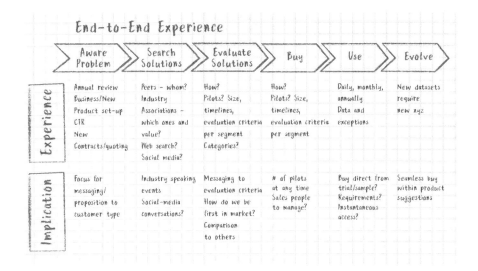

End-to-End Experience					
Aware Problem	**Search Solutions**	**Evaluate Solutions**	**Buy**	**Use**	**Evolve**
Annual review Business/New Product set-up CTR New Contracts/quoting	Peers – whom? Industry Associations – which ones and value? Web search? Social media?	How? Pilots? Size, timelines, evaluation criteria per segment Categories?	How? Pilots? Size, timelines, evaluation criteria per segment	Daily, monthly, annually Data and exceptions	New datasets require new xyz
Focus for messaging/ proposition to customer type	Industry speaking events Social-media conversations?	Messaging to evaluation criteria How do we be first in market? Comparison to others	# of pilots at any time Sales people to manage?	Buy direct from trial/sample? Requirements? Instantaneous access?	Seamless buy within product suggestions

Interview Output Canvas. It is a framework for capturing your learnings and key takeaways after each customer development session. It not only captures what you learned, but also where in the buying cycle the potential customer is. Patterns will emerge that will inform your Lean Canvas and drive GTM strategy.

Basic information. The top two fields are for factual company information. Look what you can find online before the session and ask for the rest. This will help you to see patterns and feed into your buyer personas.

- When was the interview taken? Are there any time-specific industry trends?
- Who and what job titles or positions are likely to have the problem and who aren't?
- What markets and segments are likely to be affected by the problem and which won't?
- At what company size/maturity does your problem manifest the most and what would usually be too early or too late?

Discussion summary. Outline key points of the discussion. Try to keep it to ten or fewer bullet points. During the very first conversations you might have a lot more than just ten – that is OK. Note as much information as you think is actionable.

- What are the current processes?
- What are other vendors doing in the space? Standard pricing?
- What are the main time consuming or painful areas?
- How do vendors get selected or onboarded? Who are they considering or already using today?
- What is the main, most important problem? How often does it occur?
- Where does their data come from?
- Regulations? How do they vary between different countries?
- What are the main industry/company/product/internal KPIs?
- Internal and external headcounts for current processes and/or those addressing the problem?
- What have they done to date? Why? Why not?
- What do they consider important?
- How do they differentiate themselves from competitors?
- What would an ideal world/solution/feature/workflow look like? Why? How would it be measured? When?

Key ah-has. Key ideas that surprised you, were insightful or made you change or reconsider your hypothesis. Aim for two to four key ah-has – points that will have a direct impact on your hypothesis or approach. The more business-development sessions you have, the fewer ideas will be novel to you. That is good – noticing patterns and converging on a consistent 'market view' is where you want to be, as that is where your customers will be as well.

- Non-obvious customer or user behaviour, metrics and values?
- Non-public internal priorities? KPIs? Projects? Statistics? Key drivers?
- Regulatory insight or workarounds to the most common blockers?
- Insights from recent closed-door workgroups?

- Insights, experience, opinions of your potential competitors, as seen by them?
- Insights into the company's own competitive landscape?
- Observation of emerging next-generation solutions?
- Something that you expected to be high, but it is actually low, or vice versa?
- Something that they really do not want to deal with, but still must? Why?
- Unexpected internal decision making, sourcing practices, KPIs, priorities, etc?

End-to-End Experience. Just like your sales process, the customers go through their own buying process. Your solution might be exactly what they need and well priced, but they might not be ready to buy. Or they might be past the decision-making stage regarding how they solve their problem. The sweet spot is to come in at the point at which the customer knows they have a problem and are looking for a solution. Note what you have learned about the specific customer, the stage they are at and what implication that has for you. The customer buying process is as follows:

1. **Aware (of the) problem.** Is the potential customer even aware of the problem? Is it a problem for *them*? What made them aware of it? How do they usually learn about their own problems? Is it annual reviews, employee feedback, pitches from other companies, customer requests, business metrics, industry reports? In turn, the implications for you: What is the inflection point for customers to recognise the problem? Can you create or accelerate the event or environment that causes customers to recognise that they indeed have the problem? What key area should your product description or marketing message focus on? What keywords or metrics should you use for call to action and to grab their attention?

2. **Search (for the) solution.** How does the potential customer

search for a solution? Who are the key industry influencers, peers and groups? Are there specific search platforms or product catalogs? In turn, the implications for you: At what stage does the customer start looking for solutions? How and where can you position yourself to be visible to the customer when they do? Who do you need to speak to or what groups do you need to join? On what platforms do you need to have presence? How do you start relationships with key industry events and influencers?

3. **Evaluate solutions.** Has the potential customer evaluated any solutions? What does the evaluation process look like? How large/expensive/long is it? What were previous results? What is the evaluation success criteria? Does it change with different use-cases? In turn, the implications for you: How can you meet key success metrics? How can you position yourself as better than competitors? How can you make your evaluation easy? How are you doing against your potential competitors – what is the minimum entry bar? What weaknesses and strengths can you address as compared to competitors? How can you be regarded as the best in the market?

4. **Buy.** Has the potential customer bought any products or services already? What is their buying process? How long and how much effort does it take post-pilot? Who are key people (decision makers or primary users)? How did they evaluate it over different use-cases, regions or segments? In turn, the implications for you: What features/functionality can you offer to bypass the competitive evaluation process? How many pilots can you run at the same time? How many people (engineers, sales, support, etc) would you need to support multiple pilots at the same time? How can you improve your buying process to the customer? Who and which groups internally do you need to focus on for getting product buy-in? Should you focus on a direct or partner sales strategy?

5. **Use.** How does the potential customer use the product or service?

How often? Daily, weekly, yearly? How do they handle edge cases? What is their main inconvenience or product limitation? In turn, the implications for you: How can you satisfy customer use requirements, functionally (features) and technically (scale)? How can you address competitor product limitations? How can you provide the right kind of access at the right time? How can you make the customer love your product?

6. **Evolve.** What does the next stage of the product or service look like? What and where is the potential customer looking for the future? In turn, the implications for you: How do you make it easy for the customer to learn about, upgrade and consume new benefits? What requirements do you need to prioritise today, that would support tomorrow's needs? What datasets do you need to gather today? What regulations might you need to comply with?

Follow Me Home

We honed a technique developed from 'Follow Me Home' – a concept originally used by Disney, Intuit and Apple to develop their products. We use it and a few others techniques combined to get to the heart of connecting with customers within their individual ecosystems, hopefully bringing value to all involved. The idea is to understand your customers within their own environments. This particularly resonates for software companies – understanding exactly how the user interacts with the tool in their own environment, can be very different from a sales process to get into the hands of the user.

Watching, in person, the physical and emotional reaction to your product, even to your proposition, will provide different, truer, insights that will get you to product-market fit faster. To achieve this:

1. **Identify your ideal target customer buying persona** (see 'Lean Canvas method'). At a company level first, then roles or personas that you think are an ideal fit. Do not procrastinate by trying to make it perfect with the first try – you will iterate

and go deeper into segments and roles once you have mastered the technique.

2. **Set yourself a goal of at least 30 emails or outreaches a day.** Utilise everything and everyone at your disposal – social connections, professional networks, LinkedIn messages, email address searches, etc. People have priorities and your message is likely to get lost so follow up three days after your initial contact if no response, and again five days after that. Follow-ups should be honest and tailored – you want people to feel special and not part of an automated sales funnel. Share your recent company progress or any fresh industry-relevant news that would be relevant for them too. Remember, even when you are doing everything right, 80% of customers will drop out or not respond at all. Have realistic expectations. Sometimes there are a few perfect clients that can make all the difference to your business, that you just cannot get hold of. Give them special attention – try to 'run into them' accidentally-on-purpose as they leave the office and ask for their insights. If a true conversation develops, you could even talk over a beer. Or, you could record and share a video addressed to them individually. We have seen both approaches work really well. If you do not get any response reconsider if the target customers really have the problem you think they do.

3. **Continue contacting them until you have set up your five to ten conversations.** With your initial message/outreach explain that you are doing product development, and would like to understand how they see a particular market, how that market is considered within their company and industry, what pain points they currently have and how they overcome those. Most importantly, explain that you are not there to sell, you are there to learn. Have your proposition hypothesis ready, but do not plan to share it, unless you are asked to. Ask for one hour in their own environment – you need to make

it convenient and familiar for them. Set up a video call as a second best option.

4. **Questions.** Have a list of questions that are focused on uncovering the pain points, testing your assumptions of the market and understanding the personas that you will work with – the art of good questions.

5. **During the meeting, remember it is a conversation between people, so ask questions and listen.** Probe to understand more detail and ask them to be honest. If they can't answer a question for reasons of confidentiality or unknown to them – that is OK. Resist the urge to 'sell' in a traditional sense. It's a product development conversation. Have two people from your startup in the meeting – especially for the early ones. This will give you a very well-rounded customer insight. One commercial person and one technical person works very well because each will uncover different insights from the same conversation. You do not need to use the entire meeting; don't be afraid to finish it early. The more senior someone is, the more they will appreciate short meetings. It's not time, but qualifying questions and next steps that matter.

6. **Immediately after the meeting, debrief as a team:** What did you learn? What assumptions have you confirmed or debunked? Fill the Interview Output Canvas. What implications are there for the sales process and/or for further customer interviews? Be human: send a follow-up thank you. Ensure to follow up on any actions that resulted from the conversation.

What makes the 'Follow Me Home' technique so valuable?

- **Open conversation.** When you're not focused on selling, but focused on listening, on truly understanding customer pain points, you'll quickly see how the dynamics change. The conversation is more open, consultative on both sides and can focus on solving the pain point rather than dancing around sales talk.

- **People.** We respond to *each other*, not abstract notions of a software tool. Often relationships are formed when the potential customer is interested in your startup's development and being part of a community of early users at the right time (assuming you do solve a high-priority pain point for them). The same people can later be part of your customer advisory board.
- **The learning process.** All customer (and potential customer) conversations are highly valuable. Framing their insights for shaping product development, the sales process and hiring will result in business success.

When to stop

As always, there is a healthy middle to the number of potential customers that you should be aiming to talk to. Too few and you have not learned enough about the market to make informed decisions (the Dunning-Kruger effect, a cognitive bias in which people with low knowledge of a task overestimate their wisdom). Too many and you have wasted time on learning rather than executing (the law of diminishing returns, a theory that predicts that there is an optimal level of capacity, after which adding more input will actually result in significantly smaller increases of the output). From a different perspective: 20% of sessions will yield 80% of the insights. The rule of thumb is to stop when you can predict the outcome of your next meeting ahead of time, so basically when you stop finding new key ah-has. From our experience, that happens after listening to five to ten *relevant* target customers (someone that you really narrowed down to after your early exploration) with one to three business development sessions each, over a few weeks. Be mindful if you changed your hypothesis during the process, though – a new customer segment, market, product, solution, etc would usually reset the counter.

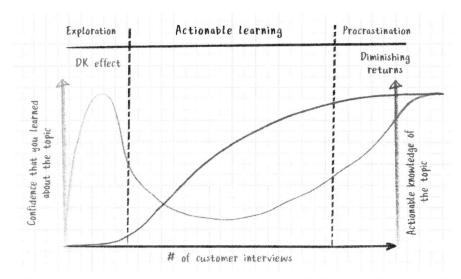

Different stages of the learning process through the business-development cycle. Feeling confident and stopping too early leaves you susceptible to the Dunning-Kruger effect bias, whereas having too many customer interviews will yield little actionable outcome due to the law of diminishing returns.

Actions speak louder than words

The goal of step two is NOT to sell or generate customers, but, as the name implies, to understand the problem. However, if your hypothesis is one of the top three priorities to your potential customers, it is likely that someone will or has already asked to do a pilot or even offered to pay for a solution. This is a good indicator that you are *looking* in the right direction and ready for the next step. If this has not happened and you just had a couple of meetings without anyone really eager to use your product, update your Lean Canvas based on the recent learnings and start over with new meetings to test the new hypothesis. From founder to founder, you would be lying to yourself if you think that customers will come if you skip this step without strong validation and just build it – they never do. However small the setback is, it is still daunting to start over, but trust us, looking back you will be very glad you did it early on saving you loads of time and frustration in the long run.

CHAPTER FIVE
Step 3: Test the solution

While starting AimBrain, everyone I spoke to – from people who have never launched anything themselves to 'industry advisors' who have seen various approaches to well-established, serial founders – was eager to advise me on the journey, and to share what *they* thought the market needs and what approach we should take. It is indeed a privilege and very beneficial to hear different opinions and experiences, however, I am definitely guilty of following advice without validation and heading in the wrong direction a couple of times. We understood the market, understood the problem, and who could be better to figure out the solution, than the customers themselves? As we learned – a very dangerous fallacy. People who have never launched a product do not appreciate how much work needs to go into it before it is even acknowledged by the industry. Their view is usually based on companies who have spent dozens of years on the market, focusing on a single solution that they themselves see and use today. Industry advisors might have been around multiple product launches and seen the process, but they've usually only observed the *outcomes*, so they usually lack the understanding behind the decision making and have little appreciation for the ugliness behind the scenes. They might have distilled decision making frameworks that can help you, but it is still up to you to give it the correct input. Serial founders, on the other hand, have done it multiple times themselves, know the process and how to apply it. From my experience at Entrepreneur First (EF), if you had two companies that were solving exactly the same problem, in the exact same industry with the exact same approach on day one, and you looked at them both one or two years later, their approaches, results and future direction would have diverged significantly from each other. Same with serial founders, they have done multiple companies and know what worked for them, but they simply are not involved day-to-day in our business and no amount of mentoring sessions can change that. It is up to you, the founder, to gather actionable insights, validate them and execute. And the only true way is to be obsessed with customers.

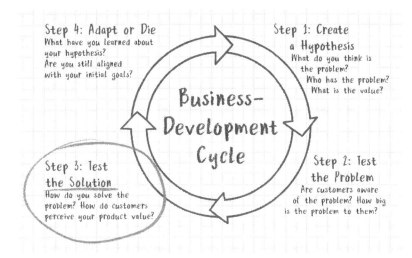

Rabbits, Deers and Elephants

Think about all the companies that you have spoken to. It was likely a spectrum including companies that varied greatly in size and in their stage of progress on their own journey. As such, they usually fall into one of the following three categories:

Rabbits	Deers	Elephants
○ Startups themselves that have likely launched within the last one to three years	○ Have a recognisable brand, and well known competitors within their space	○ Well-established brands and likely to be public (think FTSE 500)
○ Usually focused on product-market fit and growth with a single product	○ Achieved strong product-market fit and are now exploring additional verticals and solutions	○ Have multiple solutions to address multiple verticals with a strong professional services or consulting component
○ Have revenues, but likely to still rely on external venture funding to operate	○ Focused on scaling a repeatable sales model	○ Track record of expanding into new markets with new products, either through internal innovation or acquisitions
	○ Have strong revenues, and likely have significant funding rounds (>$50m) or are operating on profit	

There will always be exceptions: at AimBrain we have worked with Elephants who had very entrepreneurially minded champions, most of whom even tried to change their internal culture unsuccessfully; and we have also come across Rabbits that acted with the pride of a tier one bank in their processes, because that was the background of people who got hired there. As a general rule, you want to learn from Rabbits and Elephants, while focusing your execution on Deers,[20] because of:

- **Learning and speed.** Deers maximise value between the deal complexity, learning amount and speed. It is very tempting to go after Elephants early – we made that mistake at AimBrain – because of the potential deal size. A one-off pilot alone with an Elephant can bring in as much revenue as a contract with a Deer over a year. However, you must remember that your goal is to test your solution and the speed of each iteration is crucial. In the time it would take you to close an Elephant, you could have closed two to ten Deers, making up for the revenue by volume. More importantly, you would also have learned literally twice to ten times the amount, compared to closing a single large account. Rabbits, on the other hand, have a very fast pace, but because they are themselves not yet established, they will likely not have the volume or large user base to make it up in revenue or offer significant insights, since they are still learning about *their* customers.

- **References.** Another tempting way to justify going after Elephants is for their references and case-studies, which you could then use to bedazzle smaller customers. From our experience, references are usually just a box-checking exercise – they generally aren't enough to convince the customer to buy (do not confuse references with word of mouth!), but they can actually block a purchase if not managed carefully. We also noticed that customers feel more comfortable with references from companies closer to their own size. If a customer is asking for references before even signing a contract, you need to take that as a sign that you still do not have their full buy-in or you are against an opponent (see 'Always be validating' and Chapter Twelve). Rabbits, on the other hand, might give you the deal volume, but as soon as your bigger customers ask for the magnitude of your deployment, they will lose credibility as a reference fast.

- **Commercials**. Elephants will have dedicated procurement teams which are measured purely on the discount that they negotiate from the vendor. While in itself this sounds simple, it usually manifests in complicated commercial agreements with many stakeholders who all need to be satisfied, which means it is a slow process. On the other hand, Rabbits often buy without much structure in place at all, but change their vendors, or in fact go out of business, just as fast.

- **Operations.** Elephants usually have a huge technical dept and complicated IT systems. To add a single JavaScript line to their website often means having to coordinate with multiple teams over multiple time zones, all of which have their own KPIs, risk profiles and roadmap priorities that rarely align with your project. Before you can get even started you will need to learn about their specific security requirements (and meet them), sign off processes (and get all of them), and deployment procedures (and get prioritised as part of them, over other projects that might have been in the queue for years). From our experience it would not be unusual for this alone to take up to nine months. Rabbits, on the other hand, might not have the in-house resources needed to integrate you, or will try to save their own costs by asking you to make the full integration without expectation for the cost of professional services.

- **Focus**. Elephants will want 'enterprise' features from your product – single sign-on, audit logs, analytics, certifications, complicated user access management, strict service-level agreements and support. They are also very sensitive to any product version changes and often fall back significantly behind the current version. It is not unusual to charge £50,000–£500,000 for 'change management' professional services when the client goes out of sync with your commercially supported version – great if you are a professional services business, but a distraction if your goal is to scale exponentially. Supporting enterprise features does not add any valuable insight for your product and while professional services is an inevitable part of B2B business, it does not scale easily. Rabbits, on the other hand, will always be asking for new features and can get upset that you 'no longer pay attention to your early adopters' if you do not jump on them immediately. We have seen fellow founders *firing* customers when they become too demanding. While you do need to have a process for bringing in new capabilities, and noting customer feature requests should be part of it, you must make sure to do proper business development before you implement any of them. At an early stage you must be focused on core capabilities – the minimum viable product. Spending energy on anything else is a sure way to fail all of it.

You need to be willing to say no to certain deals and certain customers, especially at this crucial stage – you can usually go back once you are ready to scale.

Finally, the slowness due to the size of Elephants is how startups manage to overtake well-established companies with huge amounts of funding and top talent – the bigger organisation is, the more inefficient it becomes, the slower it adapts to changing customer needs, the more opportunities there are for you.

Find common patterns and prioritise

The next step is to find the common patterns from all of the business development sessions you had in order to understand your buying personas. Think about the common accelerating (keen to try a solution to their problem) and blocking (indicated that the problem is not a priority to them) characteristics. Be as specific as possible and quantify each feature. What are the common:

- Pain points?
- Sectors, industries, markets or regions?
- Types of target audience?
- Technology stacks?
- Company size (Rabbit, Deer or Elephant) or revenue?
- Needs, personalities, job responsibilities, common objections and KPIs of the individuals?
- KPIs, decision criteria or overall company priorities?
- Commercial or technical partnerships?
- Competitors?
- Channels?
- Ongoing, planned or past initiatives?

Based on the common characteristics, you want to identify the innovators – people who are willing to take a risk *today* in a non-established company just for the *possibility* that it will solve their problem (see 'What's the difference between business development and sales?'). Separate all of the companies that you had business development sessions with into groups based on the common characteristics mentioned above. Then split them into four distinct groups that represent the amount of attention they are going to get from *you*:

1. **Proactive.** These are the companies that are keen to go ahead now; the innovators. They want to hear what you are building and have explicitly asked for a pilot. They are chasing you for the latest update. The problem you identified is their number one priority and they are happy to share workarounds for their internal procurement process to get you fast tracked (e.g. what is the maximum that they can sign off without running

a Request For Proposal (RFP) process). You likely had two or three sessions with them, with strong interest and pull from them to progress.

2. **Reactive**. These are the companies that have shown explicit interest, but are just not yet ready to test an unproven solution. They wish to be updated of the progress and are happy to act as mentors, dedicate time or share strategic information until the solution is ready. The problem you identified is their number two priority and they need just a few proof points to get it done, or an event that would push the problem up to be their number one priority. You likely had one or two sessions with them, with clear next steps that require work on your side.

3. **On hold**. These are the companies that do recognise the problem, however, are not willing to invest any resources (time, money or information) in you, or the problem is not yet big enough for them. You likely had one session with them with no clear follow-up step other than keeping them updated.

4. **No go**. These are the companies that explicitly indicated that they do not have the problem and it is unlikely that they will. You likely had one session with them, with no further interest. Do mind that 'no go' is in the context of this specific hypothesis iteration. Customers from 'no go' do move to other groups sometimes (e.g. a merchant who never looked for fraud protection solutions and did not express any interest during the sessions, is now suddenly being cyber-attacked resulting in profit losses).

'Proactive', the most important group, is also the hardest group to identify. The effort needs to be led by the founders and cannot be outsourced or scaled. You are not in a position to hire any commercial people until you yourself understand what skills are required and what *good* progress looks like, which will in turn drive the commercial team's targets. This understanding will come with the first ten customers.

Even if you have absolutely no commercial experience, this is the time to get it – at AimBrain we made the mistake of hiring sales people who were very experienced in our specific industry too early. We hired them with the idea to learn from them, before having a strong understanding of the sales process ourselves, but in the end we had to just re-do everything later. Sales people cannot succeed if you don't give them the tools to do so. 'Proactive' customer group will drive your roadmap in the early days and will guide and advise you towards a 'normal' sales process (something that would be scalable as opposed to founder-driven).

The 'reactive' group is important because these will be your early adopters. You still do not have everything you need for them to buy or pilot your solution today, but this is the group that your first commercial team will look at. Adoption of this group will rely on you having at least a single proof point (e.g. a successful pilot) in a structured format (e.g. product one-pager or a datasheet). This group will not need educating or convincing, rather an explanation of how you will solve the problem. They will hand-hold you and your commercial team towards a deal. Your solution might be compared with a competitor, but a conversation or a few slides with your key advantages or differentiators will address their concerns. Experience with this group will also form the basis of your scalable sales process.

The 'on hold' group is your early majority. They recognise the problem, but would need multiple points of proof before adopting your solution. They are early in the space, compared to the rest of their industry, but the problem for them is not urgent enough and they want to follow the procurement process 'by the book'. As a startup you simply do not have time to follow their process, even more so if you are against a better-established competitor. Most of the time, when a Request For Proposal (RFP) or competitive evaluation is drawn up, the winner is already known internally, or unofficially. The rule of thumb with RFPs is a bit of an industry secret: if you or your team have not (co-)written the RFP itself or at least had enough influence to insert some 'special' mandatory requirements (something unique that only you can provide, irrespective of how much relevance it carries), it is extremely unlikely that you will win it. An RFP process requires a set number of different vendors to be considered valid and that is likely the only reason why you are there. You will return to this group once you have well-established references, case studies and a scalable sales process – which places the 'on holders' outside the scope of this book.

The 'no go' group contains the companies that do not have the problem you identified or would require a completely separate product suite to address their needs. (These companies are different from companies that do not yet know that they have a problem, which marketing would address.) What we want to do here is document our decisions and findings for this group and only revisit them if the companies release new products or branch into new verticals. Do be mindful that while the company might not have the problem, individuals do change jobs. If you impressed them by conducting yourself professionally or giving value even when you knew they were not your immediate customers, you are likely to be the first person they reach out to should their priorities change – never burn bridges.

Less is more

It can be tempting to have multiple propositions for multiple groups or buying personas early on, thinking that you will unify them later. But don't. Being defocused is a time-tested way to fail. You need to find the *biggest* pain and go after that, and only that, segment first, even if your product *could* be used by different customer types. Different verticals have different use-cases, value different things and are measured differently. You simply do not have the resources to support that in the early days. You also risk losing crucial early adopters if your marketing collateral (website, datasheets, presentations, blogs, newsletters, case studies, etc) contains too many problems and solutions that it fails to concisely pinpoint *why* and *what* you can do immediately for *them*. People have short attention spans and lots of other things to do, so if they don't see exactly what they're looking for straight away, they move on.

MVP (minimum viable POWERPOINT) versus MVP (minimum viable PRODUCT)

The minimum viable powerpoint is a vision of your product that you present to the potential customer, without actually having the product itself. It is often suggested in the startup scene to use it for validation, but remember 'The art of good questions' section. We can't tell you how many times we have seen potential customers who were in full agreement with the presentation, no matter how detailed it was, that later completely changed direction. It happens surprisingly often during the pilot integration stages too. Sometimes it is technical (e.g. an API does not work as either side expected, even though both sides reviewed the documentation beforehand, delaying the project), sometimes it is process (e.g. during mid-integrations the legal team suddenly decides to classify the information that your product collects as personally identifiable information (PII), 'just to be safe', even if they gave you a legal go-ahead before), sometimes it is people (e.g. personal priorities or goals change, delaying your project). So while it is important to have a well-documented product and processes, you should expect that you will likely need to adapt or change it as you go along based on real customer feedback, that you simply just cannot collect through a presentation, only through a real product.

Gone are the days when the sales would happen through relationships alone. Don't get us wrong, you still need to *have* one, but you cannot *rely* on it. There are so many startups trying to sell all the time, that buyers have been dulled to the flashy presentations, grandiose statements and future promises. Honesty is rare, but from our experience, pays off in the long run. Be upfront with what features you have and how you've tested them. We have seen startups that had an overall better solution, lie about a non-core capability, only to simply get disqualified from the selection process when it came down to actually delivering or testing it. It is hard to build trust, but very easy to destroy it. Be consistent with what you are sending to different customers – no matter what NDA (non-disclosure agreement) you have in place, people talk. The rule of thumb is that if you cannot build a specific capability in a week, do not pretend or position it as if you have it – manage customer expectations and build trust. Leave presentations to your future marketing team and instead focus on measuring real customer behaviour with your product in their hands.

Nail the build › measure › learn cycle

No amount of slides, meetings, focus groups, business development sessions or conversations will ever replace real users – it is simply your fear of rejection manifesting as procrastination. We know because we have done it ourselves at AimBrain, *thinking* about the next feature, rather than *listening* to customers. The purpose of the minimum viable product (MVP) is to help you validate your *direction* as early as possible, thus lowering *your* risk of wasting time, energy and money on a product that no one wants. The Lean Startup approach, distilled by Eric Ries, an entrepreneur and bestselling author, is powerful because it borrows from the scientific method: 1) create an experiment and predict the expected outcome (build); 2) run the experiment (measure); 3) compare the experimental outcome with your expected outcome (learn). You want to repeat this loop as fast and as accurately as you can:

1. **Build.** Define a minimum viable product, and at later stages a capability, given a validated problem, and ship it in small, meaningful increments (see 'Minimum viable product (MVP)'). Ask for commitment – non-paying users are *leads*, not customers.
2. **Measure**. Specify what a good user behaviour looks like and how to measure it. Monitor the metric and extract insights. Make sure

that you are measuring *behaviours* (what customers do), rather than *reactions* (how customers feel). Make sure that you build in feedback mechanisms as part of your process (e.g. weekly check-in calls), and later, as part of the product itself.

3. **Learn.** Compare your expectations with observed results. Are the results better, worse or as expected? Reach out to customers for feedback and understand what they liked and what they disliked. Why? Do you pivot or persevere? (See Chapter Six.) Be comfortable with not having a full picture – startups are all about making as few mistakes as you can with incomplete data.

Prepare to repeat the cycle multiple times until you find what really resonates with your customers.

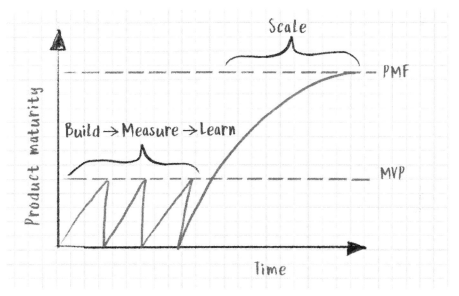

The build > measure > learn cycle over a product's lifetime. It will take multiple iterations of building the minimum viable product (MVP), measuring customer behaviour and learning exactly how to deliver the most value to them, to then scale it and reach a product-market fit.

You absolutely need to test fast, learn fast and iterate fast, otherwise you will run out of resources without having the proof points required to take you to the next level. Most investors are smart (the ones that you want as part of your board should be, in any case) and no grand vision will make up for the lack of actual measurable progress.[21] In the early days the cycle should take 80% of the founder's time; when at scale it should take 20%, and at no stage should it go down to 0%, no matter the headcount, maturity or funding of your company. Be obsessed with the customer feedback.

Minimum viable product (MVP)

Start by focusing on a single buying persona: the proactive group. You should have a clear understanding of what problem(s) they have. The next step is to define exactly *how* you will solve the problem. The **product** has capabilities and features that address specific problems and needs. How do you spend the absolute **minimum** amount of energy to solve your customer problem? What does a **viable** product that delivers *measurable* value to customers look like?

MVP does not mean it's a *simple* product or that you ship it half-done or broken. It also does not mean a landing page with a signup field, as it does not deliver any value to the customer (although this can be used to generate leads). MVP means a product that has a fully working core functionality which is *just enough* to be useful to and used by innovators. Scale at this stage does not matter – as long as you are delivering value, no one cares what happens in the background. Do things early that do not scale, if you have to.[22] However, make sure that you have a path to a product and not a services business over time.

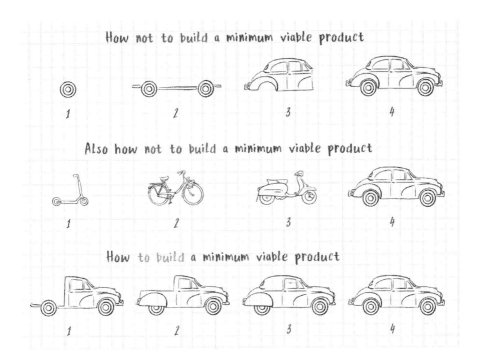

How to think about a minimum viable product (MVP). It should be something that delivers actual value to the customer from day one, and also represents a solution to the problem that meets customer expectations.

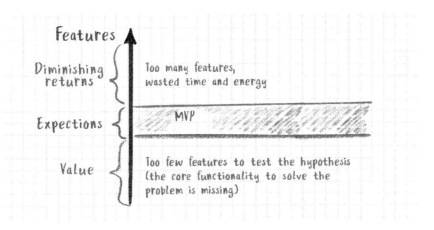

How to define a minimum viable product (MVP). Make it minimum – cut out everything that is not fundamental to delivering value. Make it viable – have just enough functionality to demonstrate value clearly.

Take the problem and define, with as few steps as possible, how you solve it and how you that translates to customer value. Note those items as product features. Compare each one to vitamins and painkillers – is it something for the customer that is nice to have, or would the customer be in *serious* pain without it? Drop the former and prioritise the latter, confirming each against the Interview Output Canvas.

Plot all your required features against two perpendicular intersecting axes: Effort (to implement) versus Return (on investment). Think about what you can do to maximise the MVP success:

- **How can you minimise the effort for individual features?** For example, if something requires high effort to automate it, technically or commercially, can you do it manually for the first few customers? If something requires a significant investment, like building an e-commerce website, can you find off the shelf tools that will cover 80% of your needs while spending only 20% of the time? Can you use UI (user interface) front-ends or libraries to deliver an 'OK' design (hint: company/UI branding is definitely not part of an MVP)? Can you manually invoice initial customers instead of setting up your entire accounting system at this early stage?
- **Is the value delivered via (deep) technology or a better workflow/UX (user experience)?** The former requires an understanding of what is possible technologically today, while the latter requires an understanding of what a good user experience *feels* like, and breaking it down into individual features. Do you have these competencies in-house?
- **Are you over engineering the product?** Trying exciting new technologies, mapping out microservices architecture that can handle 1,000 potential customers per second or refactoring code for 'maintainability' are just forms of procrastination.
- **Are you re-inventing the wheel by solving already-solved problems?** Can you use third-party services that

already exist for parts of your solution? Over time you will have the opportunity to bring all of it in-house, but only once you have validated the solution itself.

- **Are you able to release or enable parts of the solution one at a time?** For example, if you have a client-side software development kit (SDK), can you finish that and release it to the client for integration before you work on the back-end? If your product requires integration with multiple vendors, can you deliver core value with just one to start with?

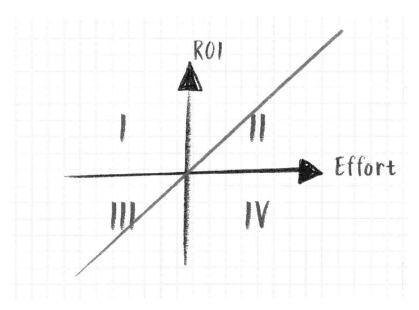

Product feature prioritisation framework. Focus on the tasks (I–IV) with the highest return on investment (ROI) and the lowest amount of effort first.

Making decisions with incomplete data to deliver the right product at the right time is an acquired skill – product sense. No amount of books will help you get better at it, only experience via repetition can. As a rule of thumb, you want to have the competency of building an MVP in-house, likely part of the founding team, otherwise it will either be too expensive or take too long to iterate.

The first quadrant on the product feature prioritisation graph is your MVP. Focus on it first and make sure you do it really, really well. Generally, you would prioritise features above the line from the second quadrant, then on to the third quadrant if you have to, almost never touching the fourth, unless it is industry regulation related.

Set yourself a realistic deadline (not too soon, forcing you or the team to all-nighters or to release an unfinished MVP, but also not too late, allowing you to procrastinate) to build your MVP, while continuing conversations with your potential customers in parallel, finding more innovators that are keen to try your product.

Make sure you know what *good* usage looks like (see Chapter Eight) and that you are measuring it. There is no big launch. Once the MVP is live with the customer, schedule a feedback session. Do not wait for them to take their time to test it. Scheduling an event in one or two weeks, depending on the overall evaluation process, will create a deadline in their mind for testing it and will generate some sense of urgency. Remember the points from 'The art of good questions' section for your feedback session. As you add new features based on your customer feedback or iterate already existing functionality (see 'Nail the build › measure › learn cycle'), think of it as *continuous onboarding* – keep your customers updated and integrate/enable parts as they are ready.

Finally, it is not the company that is first to the market that wins, but the company that is first to product-market fit. Do it right from the start and adapt to changing needs as they accumulate over time. This is also how young companies steal customers from FTSE 100 players – by the time the incumbent even realises that customer needs have changed, you will have completed ten build › measure › learn cycles (see 'Nobody else matters').

CHAPTER SIX
Step 4: Adapt or die

At AimBrain, we tried many approaches (product, commercial and team changes) until we found what *seemed* to work. No matter how many or what metrics we had, it always felt like we were choosing between doubling down on a bad idea and not giving ourselves enough time to explore a good one. Having two or three customers feels exciting, and indeed is a huge achievement in itself, but can you really scale beyond that to ten? To 1,000? How fast and how much energy will that require? Are you really tracking the right metric (see 'The North Star paradox')? To this day, I think this is one of the hardest life or death questions for the founders: *Is the startup really working?*

Back at AimBrain, we had our fair share of moments when we doubted everything. At one extreme, we had data over-engineering – overfitting our observations to the dataset and losing track of the bigger picture:

- A big bank is willing to test an unproven solution, surely everyone else will follow?
- A marketing campaign did not generate many new leads in a short time, surely we need to stop it immediately?
- On the other extreme we had an 'experience' or 'feelings' driven approach – a lot of hype but no execution:
- I have sold to financial institutions before surely I will be able to repeat that success here too?
- We have 25 banks in our sales pipeline wanting to buy us, surely it is just a matter of time?

One approach that I have seen happen too often with fellow founders goes like this: 'The average sales cycle is 6/12/24/X months and measuring anything before that is just defocusing.' The truth is in the healthy middle. It takes both metrics *and* instinct to reach it. Remember, the goal is not to go for the *right answer*, but rather to *minimise the wrong* choices. Founder instinct comes in various forms: past learned lessons (understanding why things worked the way they did, which is different from experience – if I do X, outcome will be Y, without understanding the underlying process of transforming X to Y), personal vision, commitment and excitement about specific problems or customers. Business flywheel momentum is not lost if you gracefully change the direction and continue executing. 'Gracefully' is the key word here – loss in motivation, morale or wanting to give up are the real killers.

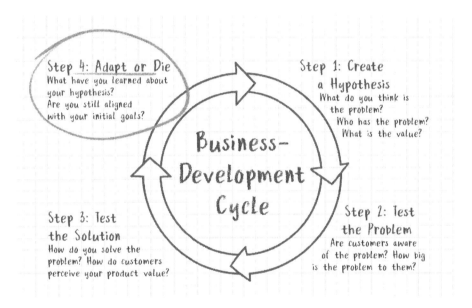

Only the *right* metrics (see Chapter Eight) can help you answer the 'when do you pivot or when do you double down on the MVP' question. A lot of metrics require scale to be meaningful – you cannot derive valid customer lifetime value (LTC) or customer acquisition cost (CAC) data until past your first ten customers. You might also already have revenue from paid pilots, which feels great and invigorates your team and investors, but remain vigilant – while a repeatable revenue is the ultimate metric, it is not representative of product-market fit in the early days and can actually be distracting, taking you down the wrong path. When scaling, things look a lot different than they did in the early days. Good early indicators that you should continue executing in the same direction:

1. **Consistency.** Are your buying persona, market, use-case and product consistent? All the steps leading up to now were about focusing on a single problem and a single type of customer. Startups are crazy and sometimes you can lose focus or go after things that feel urgent and important in the moment, but distract you from the ultimate goal – a scalable business. Is your current position still consistent with your Lean Canvas, a single buyer persona in a specific, well-defined market and a clear product scope? Are the people that you expect to get the most value from you the ones actually using your MVP the most?

2. **Behaviour.** Are the customers *behaving* as you have expected them to? Does the time from sign-up to first action, retention rate and active usage metrics still look like you expected? Do they stand up to your definition of what good looks like?

3. **Pull.** Are your customers asking for specific new or improved capabilities while still continuing to use the MVP as is? Are they asking how they can pay? Are your customers introducing you to their peers or wider internal teams? (See 'Metrics'.)

4. **Scalability.** Can the MVP be scaled through technology and automation or, at minimum, is there a path to scale in the long term? Note that even if you have a strong innovator base with banked revenue, it is unlikely that venture capitalists will be interested in investing without a clear and realistic scaling strategy.

5. **Market.** Do your market assumptions about the value created for the customer still hold? Does the customer recognise the value the same way you do? Do your customers have budgets for your product? Since learning about the market, is the addressable market still big enough for unit economics and margins to be viable? (See Chapter Thirteen.)

Counter intuitively, the goal at this stage is still not to grow, but to find a product that can grow. Getting to the first ten B2B customers that hold true for the above indicators validates your readiness for the next stage, scaling sales (a topic for another book!). Keep following the method steps and adapting when you learn new information. No matter what your company scale is, the fundamentals do not change: only metrics (i.e. what looks good) do.

The art of the pivot

And if any of the above do not hold? Then well done, you have learned what doesn't work and are on the right track to learning what does. We are using 'pivot' loosely here – it could be a small refinement to the Lean Canvas or a completely new start by throwing the canvas out and choosing a fresh idea. Pivoting can feel like failing, and I definitely felt like that multiple times throughout the AimBrain journey, but the facts are that pivoting at the right time in the right direction will compound in value over time. The opposite is also true – you might continue *trying* to scale, raise a round now, hoping that you will find a solution later or with more money or a bigger team (see ACT III). But in this case, you are working on borrowed time and it will eventually come crashing down, except with more damage to you (your brand, your professional network, your friends and co-founders, investor relationships, employee perception, mental state and personal financials). As it is said – '*smart* people find a way out of any situation; wise people do not get into those situations in the first place'. Be wise.

Think about what you proved true and what turned out to be false in your hypothesis against your Lean Canvas model:

Problem
- Have you validated that the problem you are solving is indeed a priority for your customers too?
- If your customers indeed have the problem, why is it not being prioritised?

- Is there a compelling date or event that would drive adoption? Or is it just nice to have? If the market is not yet ready, what would be the inflection point?
- Can you change your approach, language, KPIs or use-cases to make it an urgent issue?
- Is your product marketing aligned with top customer problems? For example, at AimBrain we first marketed our product as an 'authentication' solution, which no one cared about, but after we changed the marketing to a 'fraud protection' solution, conversations picked up. We did not change anything else – same people, same groups, same companies, same markets and exactly the same product.

Customer segment

- Is your product being used by the people that you have assumed it would be (as opposed to their managers, managees or different teams altogether)?
- Have you discovered that a different buying persona/segment has a higher urgency or budget for your product?
- Have you gone after generally very slow Elephants instead of Deers? (See 'Rabbits, Deers and Elephants').
- Have you focused on the right region (e.g. due to specific events or regulation, competing solutions, customer buying patterns)? What *is* the right region?

Solution

- Is your solution the right one for the problem? For example, people might revert back to using sticky notes instead of online tools to take notes, but the problem remains exactly the same – retaining knowledge.
- Have you really distilled the core functionality so that the MVP delivers value?
- Have you communicated the value and functionality clearly?

A lot of customers might not have gotten value because they simply did not know your product is capable of delivering it, or because they gave up midway because the workflow is too confusing or involved.

- Is your product sufficient on its own, as opposed to being part of a bigger product or system?
- Is your technical deployment approach right (e.g. on-device versus cloud versus on-premises)?
- Is your technical capability lacking (e.g. accuracy, speed, size, etc)?
- Are your competitors closing clients? How do they convince the market to buy? What do they have that you lack? How can you obtain it? What else can you learn from your competitor press releases, newsletters, case studies and your friendly champions (who might have spoken with them)?

Unique value proposition

- Do customers really care about your unique value proposition (e.g. highest accuracy in the class, omni-channel approach, that you can support specific use-cases, etc)? Be critical if what you think about your product matches with how it is seen.
- Are there any features that customers use heavily while ignoring rest of the capabilities? If so, you likely over-built your MVP. Focus on that feature as a product itself.
- Have you built enough to show the value to the customer? If the customers have used your product very lightly, think about whether you have missed any insights or core requirements? Revisit your Interview Output Canvas and focus on those, update your Lean Canvas and build whatever you've missed into the existing MVP.
- Do you need to partner (e.g. offer your product through a larger ecosystem or platform) or have a joint offer to provide significant value to the customer?

Unfair advantage

- Has your unfair advantage actually been useful? For example, have your insights or personal relationships generated the leads or conversations that you expected? Or has your physical location benefited you in any way?
- Have you measured your unfair advantage correctly?
- What were your expectations against reality? Why? What were the good parts?

Channels

- Are you reaching your actual target customers through the channel that you expected? Is the channel too broad or lacks specific focus? How can you 'filter' only relevant leads?
- Are your direct sales working as expected (e.g. right pricing, approach to customers and use-cases)?
- Are your partner sales (assuming you ignored our experience or it was genuinely the only channel that works in your industry) working as expected (e.g. right partners, approach to partners, commercial model, pricing, incentives and KPIs)?
- Who are you *really* competing against in the market?
- Are there any symbiotic relationships that you can tap into – situations where you winning means that your partners win too? Can you find any aligned interests?
- Is your sales approach, given a specific problem, boring and just like everyone else's?

Cost structure

- Does your proposed pricing align with customer value *perception*?
- Do costs (distribution costs like marketing, operating costs like web hosting, and salaries) look manageable and have the potential to go down over time per unit of product?

Revenue streams

- Does your revenue structure (e.g. SaaS, licence, etc) match customer expectations, habits or industry standard?
- Are you wasting energy on companies who are not able to sign off small amounts to show commitment (i.e. Rabbits)?
- Does the profit margin (difference between sell price and cost to make the product) look viable and have the potential to grow over time or with scale?

Key metrics

- Are you using the right KPIs?
- Do you really understand *why* customers are looking at you? Evaluate each customer in the pipeline and look for common patterns or language.
- Is your expectation for good customer behaviour in line with *their* expectations for the product?
- Are you measuring the customer behaviour correctly?

Big picture (expectation versus reality)

- What did you expect to happen?
- What did happen?
- Why did that happen?
- If you were to close your company today, what would your postmortem look like (i.e. imagining that the company failed and working backwards to understand what would lead to failure and how it can be addressed before it happens)?
- Do you have enough information to make any reliable conclusions for your hypothesis? Be critical of yourself, make sure to get unbiased feedback from mentors, investors and/or fellow co-founders. Review your Interview Output Canvas – have you missed any key insights?
- What did you do well?
- What do you need to change or improve?

- Does focusing only on what you did well get you where you want to be or do you need to re-plan your approach completely?
- What needs to change for short term and long term expectations? How do you measure it?
- Do you understand not only what needs to be done, but also (by) when?
- Can the current team still deliver against changed requirements and circumstances? Do you have core competencies for changed direction in-house?
- Do you have enough runway (of cash in the bank) to execute the new plan?
- Who are your key stakeholders and what do you need to demonstrate to them to get to the next stage? How do you communicate the new direction?

Adjust and start the cycle again. If it is a small change you already have a huge advantage from existing relationships. If it is a major change, be happy you discovered it now and not when it is too late. As it is said, trying the same thing and expecting different results is the definition of insanity.

Whatever the change, commit to it fully. At AimBrain we made the mistake of keeping early clients whose use-cases didn't align fully with our new direction just because 'maybe the old direction is actually good and we just need more time'. If you think that you would not have made this mistake, just know that firing a client for the first time is pretty daunting when you are up against the clock to show traction! As a consequence, we had to maintain the old product/capabilities, while testing our new hypothesis, which slowed us down immensely. We found ourselves spending time looking for solutions to keep the old clients rather than being laser focused on executing our new vision. At first, maintaining your old and new direction is 50/50, which later becomes 33/33/33 and then a 25/25/25/25 split of your energy. NOT VIABLE.

Communication

No matter the size of your pivot, a small adjustment or a completely new hypothesis, people perceive it as them being wrong, so mindful communication is crucial. People do not like being wrong nor being part of a team that is wrong. The more individuals you have in your founding and early team, the more sensitive you need to be – negativity spreads significantly easier than optimism. This is also why the rule of thumb is to build your MVP and get the first ten customers with only the founding team – people who are comfortable with uncertainty and actively seek out negative feedback because they know it is the best shortcut to greatness. Everything you build now, the culture, approach, energy – will scale and be amplified as your company scales. A toxic culture that is full of politics and individualism is not conducive towards company needs. We have seen it, front-row, from fellow founders who had product-market fit and an otherwise *healthy* business, the company to go down in flames because of co-founder disagreements or employee in-fighting. Sometimes it might be you who is the toxic one. Seek out, be open to and act on the feedback from your peers – that is the only way to grow personally.

Your primary stakeholders are you and your team. Backtracking is a significant blow to morale, especially for your engineering people, who might need to throw out very tangible work.[23] Build your culture and message around striving for real-world impact (as backed by metrics), even if that means making painful decisions short term. As Theodore Roosevelt said, 'Nothing in the world is worth having or worth doing unless it means effort, pain, difficulty…'.[24] In biological terms, only the species (read: companies) that adapt to the changing environments (read: customer and market needs) survive.[25] Effectively, it is adapt or die. When you present a change of direction, back it up with your learnings from customers: 'I feel like we should try X' comes across as weak leadership. Share your Interview Output Canvas, or better yet, you would have kept *everyone* updated on customer feedback from the beginning. Make sure that experimentation is part of the culture and people are happy to learn what does not work and understand that this brings them closer to what *does*.

Take care of your own mental state. Sleep. People perceive your body language, tone and behaviour more than you think. If you are nervous or confused about the next steps it is already communicated before you even say anything.

Have the uncomfortable conversation with your investors about your leadership – some might lose trust in you or the new direction. Not having them at the table will be more productive in the long run and being proactive allows for both sides to part on a positive note. Your goal is a scalable business and you want everyone to be aligned, heading in the exact same direction with their full force (remember the 'flywheel' concept – each step amplifies the previous one. Make sure you are amplifying the right things.)

Also consider your other stakeholders – investors. Good investors pick people rather than ideas. They understand that part of the journey, especially early, will include changing directions or even the initial ideas. They are comfortable with that – they backed you to build something great. They are also comfortable with the possibility of losing all their money and investing in you again; they know the startup failure statistics and are betting on the slim chance of something huge, otherwise they would just keep their money in interest accounts for guaranteed profit. This is also why it is important to have a relationship prior to taking their money.

It is said that 'no one wants to see how the sausage gets made, but everyone likes the result'. Your investors cannot, and likely do not want to, be involved in all the problems that happen daily behind the scenes. They will, however, do their best to help you, if you come prepared. Treat your problems as facts (without trying to make them look better than they actually are) and always have an action plan ready. Our rule of thumb is that your company events should lag by a week – give yourself time to digest what happened and understand the consequences before updating your shareholders and, if needed, asking for feedback on your action plan. Good communication with investors is the difference between being perceived as someone who is reactive and does not know what they are doing (thus unlikely to be investible again), versus someone who has their metrics in place and can steer the company forward. Investors talk and their world is small.

Finally, do not worry about customer perception when pivoting – they have their own problems – but do your best to not burn bridges. I have done it at AimBrain myself and I often see other founders keeping a legacy product or a feature alive just to save face or 'just in case we need it later'. I learned it the hard way and hope you will be wiser than me – defocusing is the fastest way to failure. Make the choice, make sure that your legals are bulletproof or you can reach a mutual agreement, communicate it and execute. It will feel shit in the moment, but will feel like a weight off your shoulders in the long term. Logistically you only have 24 hours in a day, and you should be spending them on the opportunities that can scale. History is written by the winners – what it took you to get there is secondary.

CHAPTER SEVEN
Nobody else matters
...BUT WHY YOU MUST LEARN FROM EVERYONE

Very often new founders discard ideas if they see a competitor in the space – 'It's been done already!', they say. There are also a lot of naysayers that seem to only apply their logic to startups and not to existing companies. For example, if they see a startup launching an electric car – 'not *another* electric vehicle. Copycat'. But for an established car manufacturer launching an electric car – 'amazing leadership, differentiation and stamp of approval for the market'. We were in exactly the same situation when starting AimBrain – what we were doing had already existed for 30 years. Biometric authentication was not a new concept – all the customers that we spoke to had in fact already trialled some of our competitors, sometimes multiple competing solutions. To us, this was not discouraging, quite the opposite in fact – it indicated that there was indeed a problem, but also that the existing solutions were not meeting customer needs (i.e. no customer deployments) – we were looking in the right direction. The big question to answer was – why with all of the competitors and trials, etc, had we still not seen wide adoption (or indeed commoditisation) of the technology? The answer turned out to be partially related to product performance and strongly related to market approach. Looking back, we realised that we should have spent more time learning from our competitors. One key insight that we missed was that the market-leading competitors were focused on a very specific problem (new account opening fraud), while market-lagging competitors went broad (with 'we solve fraud' or 'we do biometric authentication'). We ourselves arrived at the former message through the business development process, but we could have saved an immense amount of time and energy iterating our hypothesis if we'd learned from competitors first.

Competitors are just another tool

Many processes in a startup are flywheels, and so is the competitive market. Think about it: the bigger the market, the more competitors, the more opportunities to differentiate, which in turn attracts more customers by catering to more specific needs, making the market bigger. Starting a new market is not a battle that most startups can afford – let the competitors and incumbents educate the market, while you focus on reaping the benefits by understanding your customers better than anyone else via the business-development process. The other extreme is also true – you cannot easily win in an already commoditised market. If existing products solve customer problems well, you will find yourself competing on price, rather than value creation or innovation. Market domination will be an uphill battle that life is just too short for. Remember, the winner is not whoever is first to market, but whoever is first to product-market fit (see Chapter Fourteen).

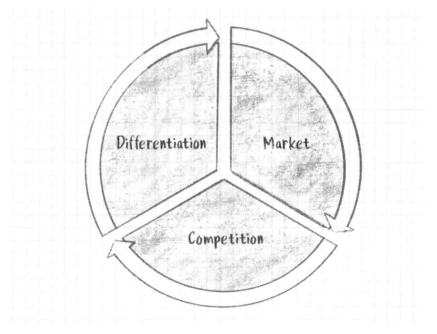

Market flywheel. The bigger the market, the more competitors will be addressing it, the more that allows for differentiation, which in turn expands the market.

Competitors are good because of:

1. **Proven market need.** Companies cannot exist without solving customer problems and capturing value (see business flywheel). However, a single company in the space is not proof of a space!

2. **Proven business model.** The longer a competitor has operated, the stronger proof for their business model is, the more buyers are familiar with it.

3. **Educated buyer.** Competitors spent energy on marketing, use that to your advantage. Teaching about a new market is really hard, showing how you are better is easier.

4. **Market experience.** Learn everything you can from competitors – what features they have, what they disabled or never launched, partnerships, channels, etc. Read their case studies, technical documentation and try any demos they offer. As the saying goes, 'Good artists copy; great artists steal.' Learn from those who came before you and make the market think that you are the leader in it.

Very, very few startups die because of competition, and even then it is probably because they did not adapt to the changing landscape. But you *must* know your competition, it will help you to iterate faster.

Know thy competition

Knowing a competitor means that at all times you have handy:

- Kill points – what strength you have against them?
- Landmines – what should you prompt your champions to ask them that you know they will not have a good answer to?

You also need to differentiate between *marketing* and *reality*. Often, competitors will market products that are not yet ready, or features that do not yet exist, as a marketing exercise. The customer is the only truth you need to care about – ask for their experience or expert intuition about competitor offerings. Chances are they have tried the solution and/or have non-public insights about it (see Chapter Eleven). We have also seen instances where potential customers would announce publicly that they are working with our competitor, where it turned out to be simply not true. Rather, it was an agreed press release *before* a pilot, that in fact ended up going poorly. Most of the information is noise, so speak with your customers to find out what's really going on. Do not cross them off the list until you verify facts personally – treat such occurrences as an opportunity to learn from the mistakes of your competitors – be *wise*.

Understand where you are strong and where your competitors are weak:

- **Website, video demos, industry conferences, demo apps and accounts.** Break down what is happening and why: What is the workflow, UX and UI? Why is it like that? Why are some steps skipped and some enforced? Is it just a demo or does it apply to the real product too?
- **Press releases and investor news.** Read through past releases – are they still heading in the same direction? Any product launches that no longer exist? Any mentions of their specific market focus? Are they still in those markets? Why/why not? Are they focused on a single problem or a wider market? Recent acquisitions and the impact of these on direction? What keywords/calls to action do they use? How has that changed over time? Investor reports – technical/financial performance? Future goals/direction?
- **People**. Use LinkedIn. How big are their sales, marketing, support, research and development teams? This can give you an indication of whether the product is being built in-house versus a reseller/partnership focused approach. The former gives flexibility to move with a changing market landscape, while the latter makes them dependent on third-party vendors.

If a company is positioning themselves as deep-tech, do they have the team to back it up? Does the team have research credentials? Recent hires or fires? Strategic employees, investors or advisors with past industry experience?

- **Headcount.** Number of employees and month-on-month headcount growth rate? Headcount is a proxy indicator of company growth (would you bet on a company that is expanding or contracting?). Do they have enough operational people to support service-level agreements? Regional coverage – what regions are they focused most on? In what regions do they have a local presence or office and what teams (sales, technical, support, etc) are based there?

- **Analyst reports.** Find analyst reports for your market. What are the past and future trends? Who are the current market players? What are their differentiations as seen by the market? Why did specific vendors get mentioned while others left out? Any vendors that got removed from new analyst reports that were present in the previous ones? Why? Change in market needs or vendor direction?

- **Patents, publications, scientific conferences.** Read patent summaries, understand what is being claimed – there might be insight into *how* certain things work or the directions that company is or will be taking (account for patent recency). If a company is heavy on establishing intellectual property publicly, see if there are any marketing claims that are not backed by patents?

- **Monitor their movement.** You want to always have up-to-date information and spend some time understanding implications when significant events happen. Subscribe to their newsletter, Crunchbase notifications, Google Trends or similar. Set up uptime monitoring on their main assets – are there any maintenance patterns? Outages?

Resist the temptation to say anything bad about your competitors, privately and especially publicly, because this will come across as arrogant, and it's not productive. Everything you claim needs to be verifiable, ideally by being in the public domain (press releases, customer case studies, research, etc). Avoid unsubstantiated claims like 'better malware detection' – how is better defined? How is it measured? As compared to who? In what circumstances is it better? Statements like that boost your ego, but do not really deliver any value to the customer. Focus on quantifying *how* your features or products solve customer problems instead. Furthermore, do not confuse your customers by showing them capabilities-comparison graphs either. Always think how your competitors can flip your arguments. For example, say you have a competitor that is well established in the e-commerce sector, while you are experienced in banking. You are both going after the same banking customer. You might use the argument 'we have better data and performance because we are focused on banks'. A competitor can flip it by saying 'e-commerce experience gives us better data as it is diversified over different customer types and fraud which drives better insights overall'. You just lost by not being specific and using unverifiable claims. Better to focus on facts: 'we have been deployed in a competitive scenario with the vendor in question and outperformed them on X metric as measured by Y'.

Finally, we have seen instances when a competitor claimed something that was just not possible or likely. Don't worry – customers are not stupid. That competitor might succeed in getting a few pilots early, but the market talks and soon they will be known as a company that cannot deliver against their promises. If you do this, it makes it unlikely that anyone will pilot you again, even if you pivot in the future. Individuals also move jobs and will remember you as that company's founder. So never lie – trust (in your brand) is very hard to build and very easy to lose.

CHAPTER EIGHT
Know your early metrics

...AND HOW TO KNOW WHEN IT'S WORKING

It is an amazing sight when the whole company is aligned and working towards the same goal – you can feel the magnetic energy in the room.[26] Choosing KPIs is easy – what we learned at AimBrain is that choosing the *right* KPIs is hard. If not challenged, the company will often base its processes on everyone's past experiences, likely in many different directions, against your vision and immediate priorities. This will drive wrong behaviours while *feeling* 'productive', essentially wasting precious energy. For example, we set ourselves a goal to increase self-service signups on a week-on-week basis by 5%. We achieved that – our numbers went up, the plots looked beautiful and we felt good about ourselves. The problem was, however, that product usage did *not* follow. We chose a vanity metric; we measured, and thus optimised, the wrong thing. We later shifted to measuring two metrics: a product metric – time to the first API call – and a growth metric – number of active users, defined as someone who made at least ten API calls in the reporting period. We got there eventually, but it cost us valuable time and energy to adjust our approach and re-align everyone on the team. Remember, people do not like being wrong. Setting the correct KPIs by understanding what good and bad performance looks like is vital early on. It will help you not only to drive the *right* behaviour, but also to know when you should evaluate new strategies or when to double down and scale the current effort (see Chapter Six). If the product-market fit is about building the *right thing*, then the sales process is about scaling the right thing right, and you can only do that by measuring the *right* metrics.

In the 'Why do startups fail?' section we argued that there is a healthy middle ground between no planning and over-planning. The same exact idea applies for business development KPIs: when faced with certain outcomes or achievements, pessimists will quit too early, while optimists will tend to drive the effort, draining already very limited energy too far, believing that they need 'just one more thing' to hit success. If you give up too early you will be just another founder who quit and lost your shareholders' money, however, if you continue with your rose-tinted glasses on, ignoring signs that you should change something, you will end up as just another 'zombie startup' (one that is neither gaining traction nor fully dying – a position often considered as worse than simply failing and starting fresh)[27] in your shareholders' portfolio. Neither is good and in both cases, you, the founder, will likely burn out mentally. I know I did at AimBrain.

It is important to base your decisions on metrics that *actually* matter (see 'The North Star paradox'). Think about the exponential curve – in the early stages the growth is very slow, and then it explodes.[28] The right metrics early will help you see trends and insights that indicate whether your hypothesis *can* grow. The right metrics will be specific to your market and customers, who will also help to inform the upper and lower bounds of how 'exceptional' and 'poor' performance for a company in the space looks like, as well as the time frames in which it would be reasonable to achieve certain growth goals (usually dictated by the buying cycles). Finally, different stakeholders, including yourself and your employees, will have different KPIs that feed to improve your specific metrics. It is important to make sure that KPIs are communicated to everyone, kept updated and follow S.M.A.R.T. criteria: Specific, Measurable, Attainable, Relevant and Time-framed.

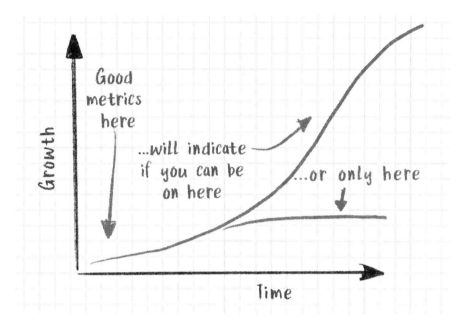

Exponential startup growth curve. The right early metrics are a key indicator for future growth and will guide you if you should continue or change directions.

Company KPIs

As a founder you must, at all times, know your KPIs around the following:

1. **Customers.** Know your current customers, their status in the pipeline, next steps and next immediate customers. Prioritise and execute like fuck. Communicate the progress and customer needs, priorities and requests weekly within the team to keep the business flywheel spinning to maintain a sense of urgency. Ten enterprise customers is enough to get you that next big round of funding to kick into sales scaling mode. Focus on the 37% rule in the 'Idea generation' section: get a list of more customers than you think you will need, accounting that some will be busy, some won't be ready right now, and some just won't fit into the 'Time' metric below.

2. **Usage.** Know how your customer is consuming your product. Which customers are ramping up your usage naturally and why? How can you replicate that? This will drive your insights for the next ten to 1,000 sales.

3. **Value.** Know your value to the customer and how the value exchange works – the economics of the problem that you are solving. Remember, it is not about how much they are paying you today – your first few customers will likely be via one-off paid pilots.

4. **Time.** Your runway and options for extending it. Always know your options – you will likely have to deploy at least one of them at some point. R&D credits, research grants and side consulting are all great ways to extend your runway. Be mindful of being distracted by them, or thinking that a 'strategic' grant or engagement will lead to actual customers – unlikely.

You cannot improve the things you don't track. Do not overcomplicate things with Salesforce in the early days – a simple Excel/Google spreadsheet will do the job. You will evolve the sales pipeline and process over time to match your customer buying patterns. Share the spreadsheet within the company and always have it ready when you are meeting with investors. Make sure any key statistics or metrics are automated within – you don't want to be wasting time creating presentations. Your time is best leveraged talking with customers. As a rule of thumb, if the snapshot of your core metric graph remains true for more than a week – you are not making enough progress or the metric is too abstract.

Pilot KPIs

Commonly the terms 'proof-of-concept' (PoC) and 'pilot' are used interchangeably. They both mean that your product will be evaluated by a customer. However, they have a significant difference in *how* the evaluation will be done:

- A PoC implies a 'lab' testing setup with fake data or internal employees *playing* around with the solution. The goal is to demonstrate the concept without evaluating it in a real-world scenario, often to save time and costs. This is great, in theory, for the customer. In reality, it handicaps you both.

  From your perspective, fake data is useless and any behaviour that you will observe will be artificial. You will not gain any significant *actionable* customer insights. Remember, your goal is to iterate the build › measure › learn cycle (see 'Nail the build › measure › learn cycle') as fast as possible, and PoCs defocus you from that. It feels great to have the customer company logo in your sales pipeline, but provides no useful outcome.

  The customer, on the other hand, will lose value inadvertently. PoCs do not require production integration or team training, which means that the whole process is much less rigorous. It also likely involves only a single team, which means that your PoC will be just an internal to-do item, as opposed to a planned company or team deliverable. As a consequence, your product might not get the attention, time or thought it needs to really show value. When that happens, it is usually your fault for not communicating its value clearly enough, however, with the first ten customers you are still learning *what* and *how* to communicate. A less-than-ideal evaluation report might be the difference between the customer progressing with you and the customer taking a look at your competitor. Customers feel good for saving costs and time short-term, but you (and they) risk the chance that they will pass on a product that could have saved them significantly more in the long-term.

- A pilot implies small-scale *production* roll-out. It can be limited to a region, channel (e.g. mobile versus web banking), platform (e.g. Android versus iOS) or user cohort (e.g. customer beta testing group). The key point is that the product is evaluated with real users (can be customer employees too, if that is your user-base) in real-world scenarios. Pilots are more complex, require a significantly harder integration and longer time frames, but are absolutely what you should be aiming for. If the customer refuses to do a pilot, they are likely not your innovators and should be moved from the 'proactive' to the 'reactive' group (see 'Find common patterns and prioritise').

Going straight to a pilot instead of a PoC will signal customer validation (see 'Always be validating') and help you to understand what process to expect with your future customers.

It might feel uncomfortable to charge your first customer for a pilot, after all they are taking a risk on you and giving *you* the data and references, but you must go in with the attitude that you are worth the fee. Humans value something as *lesser* if they obtained it for free. It also further validates their commitment and creates a measure of urgency to use that which they paid for. Interestingly, the more you charge, the more value customers perceive in your product (see the market supply and demand model: psychologically, items of higher price are perceived to have higher value and are thus in higher demand as well).[29] Conversely, if you charge too low it will signal to your competitors and customers that your product is either immature or does not have significant traction. Remember, people talk.

It might be tempting to fill your pipeline with unpaid 'strategic' pilots. In our experience nothing good ever came out of these opportunities. Consider for a moment: if there is no set budget to solve a problem, does the problem really exist or is it big enough?

From our experience, expect to charge £10,000–£30,000 for small-medium businesses (Deers) and £50,000–£100,000 for large enterprises (Elephants) per pilot, depending on the value that you create for your customers (which is to be measured as part of the process). Make sure you have justification for a specific price figure. Aim to fix the upper bound as the maximum amount that your customer can sign-off without additional internal oversight, and the lower bound should be proportional to the time and effort required from your side. To gauge the former, genuinely just ask them what that amount is and position it that you usually charge more, but because you are really excited to work with them, you will discount the pilot price to that amount – start collecting that positive karma. For the latter, set a daily rate for the time and materials of your expert team (e.g. £1,000/day) to make sure that you have covered the resources needed for the success. Either way, make sure that the specific amount is justified by a *measurable* value created for the customer. Look for additional opportunities within the same business – explore different business groups, use-cases or channels, leveraging the existing relationship and operational setup. Remember, you only can run a limited number of pilots at any given time and that there is an opportunity cost to you.

NEVER EVER start a pilot without time-bound KPIs of what success is for both you and the customer, and what the next steps look like if you meet it. At AimBrain, we got stuck in this trap. Multiple times. Customers signed pilot agreements, and we fulfilled the usage and value metrics, but unfortunately the timing component was too slow. Enterprise customers are full ecosystems in their own right and without clear next steps as part of the pilot agreement, it might take them a couple of months to even come to a conclusion about whether the pilot was a success or not. You cannot afford to waste time in the same way.

Use S.M.A.R.T. (Specific, Measurable, Attainable, Relevant and Time-framed) criteria that aligns with your usage, value and time metrics. You should have a good understanding of what they are from your customer interview sessions: agree them *together* with the customer and write them down as part of the pilot agreement. This way, both you and the customer, can hold each other accountable. Think and note what *you* need in order to show value and validate your hypothesis:

- What is the minimum amount of data or interaction that the customer needs to provide?
- How many sessions/uploads/item additions, etc, will the customer need to do?
- Which of your customer's internal teams will you need access to? Engineering, operations, etc.
- How much time will you need to train/set up/calibrate before showing results?

And guide the customer home by thinking of what *they* need to enable the pilot:

- Does your champion, and thus you, have all relevant business unit buy-ins?
- Does your champion (and thus you) have the pilot budget unlocked already? Is there any documentation required to unlock it?
- Does your champion have integration resources unlocked? Teams, access, clearance, etc. Do you need to provide any supporting documentation?
- Who or which team is most likely to be a blocker? Why? How can you show value to them?
- Do you hold the required legal or security certifications? Very often customers will ask for industry certifications (e.g. ISO/IEC 27001, SOC, etc), but this is not something that you even want to consider at this stage – it simply takes too long and costs

too much. Always ask for an internal risk assessment evaluation as a way around it. This is usually an extensive questionnaire making sure that you adhere to best practices. From our experience, with the right answers to this internal risk assessment, even tier one banks and the largest credit card companies are content to progress with it in the absence of official certification.

Double confirm your assumptions by asking your customer directly what they would need to see in order to progress to a purchase. The success criteria need to be S.M.A.R.T. and will be dependent on your specific situation, but you need to quantify how it leads to:

- **Saving costs.** Reducing operational overheads, materials, employee time; removing manual labor by introducing automation, etc. Be mindful to position your product as something that *enables* people rather than *replaces* them. The latter can be viewed negatively depending on your target audience.
- **Increasing revenue.** New customers, new business opportunities; existing customer upsell opportunities, etc. Be able to explain it clearly to the customer – know the economics around your proposition and what that translates to from their point of view.
- **Saving time.** Indirect cost savings or increased revenue by optimising existing processes, upgrading tools, technologies, frameworks, workflows, etc to save time. For example, a product that shortens time to process a banking loan application means that the same workforce over the same period can now process more customer requests. While you do not bring new revenue directly (no new loan requests brought by you) nor save any costs (customer is keeping the same workforce), your product does indeed deliver significant *measurable* value. From our experience, time optimisation is hard to measure and sometimes prove.

- **Regulation.** Items, changes or functionality that companies are simply forced to adhere to by the regulatory landscape. For example, EU PSD2 SCA (a requirement for electronic payments to be performed with multi-factor authentication to reduce risk of fraud) created many new cross-sell opportunities for existing fraud protection vendors in the market (existing product adapted to a new channel). However, be very conscious of relying too much on this category – customers tend to care more about box-checking (i.e. doing the absolute minimum to satisfy the requirements) than the actual product in these situations. They might indeed implement your product, but the situation is unlikely to yield significant learnings or scale opportunities for you. Regulation changes all the time and if you are not seen as a proper product, just a way to tick a box, it makes it very hard to upsell.

The bottom line is that you need to treat the pilot like a real business deal on its own, and plan accordingly.

CHAPTER NINE
Running a successful pilot

Even as a first-time founder, my expectations of the customer buying cycle were extremely naive: Surely, I thought, if I can just get customers to agree to pilot our product, they will see how great it is and will want to buy it, and I can get on with the next pilot? Energy-costly mistake. While we did not have the volume of customers to draw any meaningful statistical conclusions, it is safe to say that early on only one in five pilots would transfer to a paying customer. It took us a few pilots that did not convert to start really exploring and understanding what was happening and to define a pilot-to-production framework around future engagements. Since we nailed down the process, we have not lost a single opportunity once at pilot stage. Do note that we exited AimBrain around the same time – it would be very optimistic to expect such conversion to last over a longer period.

Pilot-to-production agreement

The most important point of all, is that you agree with the customer on what happens in the event of a successful pilot (as shown by your jointly defined success criteria, see Chapter Eight), hence the 'to-production' part! First of all, in order to understand the customer you need to ask for facts, past behaviours and discard any hypotheticals and emotions (see 'The art of good questions'). Pilots are specific to product and industry, but at a minimum, try to understand past customer successes and failures:

- **How do they usually purchase products?** Is there an internal process they could share with you? Perhaps anonymised or full reports from past pilots that you could review?

- **When was the last time the customer evaluated a product like yours?** Are they actively looking to buy or just doing exploratory research? Did they buy the product after the pilot that time? Do they usually run many pilots and pick a winner or just one or two, which indicates they are mostly looking to validate their choices? The former might indicate that your time is better spent elsewhere, while the latter suggests that the pilot is yours to win.

- **How long does the customer usually run the pilots for?** Is the time frame driven by the product, their evaluation requirements or an internal process? Understand and address what blockers you might have *before* they even come up.
- **How did the last few pilots go for your customer?** Were they successful or unsuccessful? Why? What was good about them? What did the customer really dislike? What would they do differently this time? Why? Just like you, customers are also in a continuous learning process – be *wise* and learn from them. Incorporate the positive parts and preempt the negative ones.

End-to-end process. Setting good pilot KPIs is crucial, but it's only a part of the overall process. If you want a successful pilot, you need to understand what one looks like and guide your customer home at each step, hence the 'end-to-end' part! How will you onboard the stakeholders? What resources your customer will likely need? Ongoing deliverables? Time frames for interim milestones? Fundamentally, think what project planning your customer will need to do it, and do it for them – guide them home. Make sure to outline these things week-by-week as part of the agreement. Customers will appreciate you doing the heavy lifting and making them look good in the project. Ask if they have a standard pilot template that worked really well in the past that you could use – position it that it will be easier for *them* if you adapt that to the pilot, rather than sending a completely new document that they, and their legal team, are not familiar with. Your goal is to create a time-bound step-by-step guide that everyone can follow, which has periodic touchpoints and leads to success.

Design phase. Make sure that you include a design phase at the start of the pilot. This is your time buffer to learn any technical integration details and to customise your product for the specific customer. Make it clear what resources you will need from the customer and, just like the whole process, make sure this stage has clear time boundaries.

Realistic expectations. From the business development process you should have a good sense of what the customer expectations/KPIs are for your product. Validate them with your champion and double check with your team if they are realistic in this specific pilot scenario (i.e. your capabilities, workload and resources against time restrictions). Remember the business flywheel? Success is everyone's responsibility, and so is failure. Never go rogue and commit to stuff that your team doesn't believe it can deliver, hoping for some magic to happen. It never does.

Pricing. Sometimes, even after agreeing the pilot pricing verbally, the customer will ask for a discount due to pressure from their finance or procurement teams. If pilot price becomes a blocker do not discount it, as that is part of your market validation, but offer to offset the pilot amount against commercial subscription/contract/licence, etc – you should have enough margin there anyways. You are meeting them in the middle, but also being firm in the value that you believe the product will deliver. Some customers get creative and ask for the pilot to be refundable if it is not successful. Explain that you are here not to test if your product works, but to show what value it brings to them, and that a quality process requires resources on your side.

Intellectual property. Absolutely make sure that you own any and all intellectual property that is created as part of or as a consequence of the pilot (i.e. derivatives of customer data, computer models, know-how, designs, etc). Pay special attention to situations where you use client data to build algorithms that will be used commercially with other customers. This might come up during investment due diligence and will cause issues down the line, when it is not clear if what you built even legally belongs to you. While it does not prevent you from continuing your business on a day-to-day basis, at later-stage funding rounds (Series A onwards) or when you have an exit event (an IPO or an acquisition) it will definitely come up as a show stopper. Walk away from the pilot if the customer is not happy with this.

Next steps. The goal of a pilot is to demonstrate the value that you claimed your product will bring. Naturally, if that is achieved as per jointly defined success criteria, the relationship should progress to the next stage, a commercial agreement. Make sure that you work with your champion to set expectations in writing as part of the pilot agreement, on the subject of a commercial contract (see Chapter Twelve):

- **Commercial budget.** Does the customer have a dedicated budget for your type of product or problem solution? It is not about asking the customer to commit to a specific figure, which would be premature, but rather to understand if there is a budget, *how large* it is and what the process is for unlocking it.

- **Commercial pricing.** Customers will usually ask for pricing part of pilot negotiations, but in case they do not, raise it yourself. Do not progress to pilot until they have agreed with preliminary pricing that lines up with their budget, the value created and your expectations – both sides need to be comfortable with the next stage.

- **Roll-out strategy.** What does a full roll-out look like? Who needs to sign it off? Any new relationships that you will need to make (e.g. with specific procurement teams)? What are the usual time frames? What are the past successes and failures of vendor roll-outs?

- **Volumes.** What volumes are they seeing now? How will that change over time? What are the main drivers and KPIs for them?

- **Time frames.** What are the usual time frames involved when negotiating legal contracts, unlocking all resources and going from a successful pilot to a commercial agreement? What drives those timelines? What are the past successes and failures?

During the pilot

Handholding. You must make sure that you are involved in each step of the pilot process – only then will you gain *actionable* insights. It does not work via proxy (your champion). Think about the training materials or internal announcements for your product. Offer to write them yourself, or at least to review them, and actively seek feedback and stay in the loop. Be mindful of industry terminology and specific call-to-action trigger words. Will there be training sessions? Make sure you are running them, rather than your champion, or at least offer to be on-site if they need any help.

Interim reports and status updates. Your goal is to deliver value to the customer and you should start doing that even before the pilot concludes. Make sure to set up periodic touchpoints that align with your customer KPIs to share up-to-date metrics and to create opportunities for you and the customer to raise any potential issues early. From our experience, weekly meetings work well – if there are no issues or agenda items from either side, make sure to still share the metrics, even if it is just a ten-minute meeting. Always go to their offices (and have a dial-in option for people who are not present) – this will build rapport much faster and you could gain unexpected insights person-to-person, outside of the meeting room.

Onsite support. Dedicate an engineering integration or onsite support resource from your side, who is present on a weekly basis for at least a few hours, at the customer premises. In the early days this should be one of the founders. Talk with the people who are doing the actual evaluation, to immediately address or fix any issues. This will build rapport with them and allow you to learn the company politics, enabling you to better navigate them in the future. Listening to the customer is time well spent.

Preemptive action. ALWAYS monitor your pilot progress with all stakeholders, including your own team. Shit happens. If you see any indication that you might not meet the success criteria put a plan in place immediately to address that. Do you need more time? More data? A larger user-base? Raise it with your champion as soon as possible. Position it to their advantage, saying that the changes will lead to better results overall. If you wait until the pilot concludes, it is unlikely that you will be given another chance and it will leave a negative mark on your brand. Remember, people talk.

Post-successful pilot

References. There is no better proof of success than a positive reference from someone who is actually *using* your product. 'Using' being the keyword here. Ask your champion for references for your future customers or investors. Be mindful that you ask for it at the right time. Too early and a reference of 'Yes, we piloted the product and results were positive' will actually raise doubts – why are they not *buying* it? A good early reference should cover the positive pilot outcome and display the customer's progress towards actually buying your product.

Press releases. There is a lot of noise in enterprise space and your company needs to cut through it. Getting your logo in front of potential customers creates brand familiarity (however, note that being aware of a brand is different from taking action with that brand – that's why sales and marketing are different processes). As you are likely being evaluated by a larger company they will often have their own internal or outsourced public relations (PR) team with an extensive industry-specific network. Ask your champion to leverage their expertise to show off your (joint) success publicly – it will act as social proof with your next customer and will be acknowledged by potential investors, often by them reaching out to *you*. It is likely that the **PR** team can do a better job than you in composing a professional press release, but make sure to be involved in the process – tailor your product description to your target audience. Include as much *quantifiable* information (value added, costs saved, etc) as your customer is comfortable with sharing. Tell your customer that the success of your company means you will be able to support their needs even better in the future, so it is in their interest to help you (in this case by letting you publish useful information on a press release). Make a note to follow up with another press release once the customer signs the contract to increase your brand repetition. That being said, there are situations where you may want to fly under the radar for as long as you can, especially in the US due to potential patent trolls (speaking from experience). Legal litigation at an early stage will kill you, irrespective of the claimant's case validity. Remember, press releases are only a *bonus* – being 'famous' is a consequence of good execution, so make sure that you are not being distracted by them. Finally, never read the publication comments.

Venture arm. Does the customer have its own venture arm? If so, now is a good time to ask for an introduction, with successful pilot results in hand. Do mind that you are unlikely to want to take corporate money at this stage and, moreover, it is unlikely that you have made enough progress for them to be seriously interested. But having external interest (remember, people talk!), or even a competing term sheet, will definitely improve your next round's offer terms with whomever you decide to raise (see Chapter Fifteen). Your goal at this stage is to create relationships, even if it is a single call to understand how their process works.

It is not your baby. Early pilots are especially strategic. Executing them well, learning from them and iterating is literally the difference between the life and death of your company. It will be emotionally hard to throw away what you have built, if you learn that it is not required by the customer, or if you built something overly specific to a single customer, but don't get attached. Time is scarce and focus is the name of the game.

Pilots that do not progress. Sales are all about relationships (see Introduction and Chapter Eleven). You have defined success criteria, and met them, only to hear 'Our internal priorities have changed'. To your surprise, a few weeks later, you also see your customer using your competitor instead. What happened? Most likely you have not built a good enough relationship with your champion. A 'change of priorities' simply means that they are not willing to share the real reason behind their decision and are no longer invested in your success. Customer priorities do sometimes genuinely change (ignoring for a moment that they are now using your competitor instead), but then the liability is with you for not validating it deep enough early in the business development process – there are always subtle leading indicators, 'red flags', of coming change, you will learn to notice them with experience.

Learning what did not work

Even if you follow the process to the letter, deliver what you promised, do your best to get everyone's buy-in and sniff out any red flags, it still *will* go wrong sometimes. Shit is bound to happen that is within and often outside of your control. As the title indicates: you didn't fail, but instead gained potential insights into what doesn't work. There is no space for blame (self, customer and especially your team members) and there are no shortcuts – you need to actively reflect on what you can improve for future engagements:

Product. Was it a random one-off product event that caused the pilot to go wrong? Even if you think it will not happen again, what can you do to *make sure* it does not? Have you delivered all promised functionalities? Was your product easy to use/setup/onboard? Did you succeed in proving your product value, as seen by the customer?

Learning something new about the product is great as in the early days it is exactly your goal to iterate it to reach a product-market fit.

Process. Did you understand the customer-buying process fully before following it? Did your process facilitate all stakeholders delivering on their promises (resources, time, prioritisation, etc)? Was your process clear enough and useful to the customer? Did you fully understand all your customer requirements, other than simply the product functionality? Why and where does your customer think the pilot went wrong? What process steps can you add/amend/remove to minimise potential future issues? Learning something new about your process is good, early days it is very much an exploration (business development) until you refine it for scale (sales).

People. Did everyone on your team act professionally? Were individuals constructive during the process, suggesting how to improve different aspects of it, rather than simply declaring that it will fail (which becomes a self-fulfilling prophecy)? Were you clear about the process with everyone internally and were everyone *enabled* to follow it? Did you take input and suggestions constructively and acted on them? Learning something new about people is good, but only if the people involved want to improve. It could be a potential issue if that is not the case – the founding team needs to be exceptional at execution and constantly seek out to better themselves. Founding team's mindset will form the basis of company culture and will be amplified by future hires (see 'Build the founder mindset').

Even if the pilot went very wrong – do not feel bad for 'wasting' your customer resources. While it is unlikely that they will give your product another go immediately, you will definitely be able to revert back at a later time, once you have multiple successes with other customers. Risk of pilots failing is an already accounted part of doing business and evaluating new products. Once you have reflected and think you know *what, where* and *why* went wrong, circle back to your customer to validate your assumptions. Be thankful for the opportunity you had – do not burn any bridges, even if you think it was all their fault.

While it is important to learn at every opportunity, be careful to not generalise from a single event, look for patterns instead: is it a specific customer size/use-case/sector/timing that is proving to be a challenge? Do you usually stumble at the same business development/sales/pilot/ deployment process stage? Iterate your product and/or process and move on to the next customer. It is impossible to win them all.

CHAPTER TEN
Understanding why customers leave

Every time a customer left us, it would hurt. 'We did everything we *thought* we should – why do they not love us?' This feeling would ripple through the company and lower the morale. Over time at AimBrain I learned that customers leaving you does not necessarily mean they didn't like our product, and almost certainly does not mean they have any issues with us personally. It is an intricate balance between their changing needs, the landscape around them and, frankly, their own internal politics.

Customers leaving (a process of churn) is a fact in all businesses. By working hard on your business development process early on, it lays the foundation for accountability, and more importantly, constant improvement. It must be part of your company DNA (organisation's culture and strategy) – correct systems (for example, a culture focused on tracking results rather than inputs) allow for B players to become A players. One of the key advantages a startup has is speed and adaptability. Great founders understand that today's performance is a *result* of the work from many months before, and they are always focused on adapting to changing market needs. This is the reason why no matter the size of your business, you must always allocate time for talking directly with your customers.

Churn is a *consequence*, an outcome, of your product not meeting customer needs. Those needs can change over time and so can the target customers. Hope is not a strategy – retention will *not* improve on its own (see ACT III) and trying to repeat what worked before and hoping for different results, is a definition of insanity. What a *good* customer behaviour looks like will be very specific to your business and can change over time.

Sometimes customers will leave simply because their *circumstances* change, rather than their needs or your delivery. There is not much to learn from that, unless this is happening at an increasing rate, at which point you need to look at your market trends and potentially rethink target customers.

Either way, your goal is to *always* know what works and why for your active users and what needs improvement for your lost customers. Never be upset with customers who leave – they are an invaluable source of information for you to learn from, often an even more informative source than some of your existing customers. From our experience, if you offboard them well (e.g. provide all the data they asked for, help with technical transition or potentially make contractual exceptions) they indeed might return to you in the future. Often, customers just stop using your product, without seeking an alternative, while still paying for it. This is why revenue, a *lagging* indicator, is not the best growth KPI, especially early on. For a customer to switch, it takes energy and, more importantly, the admission that they made a wrong choice. So when it happens, it implies that the competing solution offered higher ROI even when accounting for onboarding and the cost of losing face. In either case, there would have been early signs that you should learn to look for:

Track it all. It is crucial to have a hypothesis of what a good customer behaviour looks like and track it. Additionally, aim to track as many quantitative behaviours as you can – the definition of 'good' changes over time and having supporting metrics can help spot new patterns or validate your primary KPIs. Lay the groundwork for scale (see 'Constantly evolve success metrics').

Success is everyone's responsibility. Involve your technical leaders in business meetings or calls, even if in listen-only mode. The goal is for them to understand what good customer behaviour looks like from a *technical* point of view. They will also have a different perspective and are well positioned to challenge your assumptions. What is the customer asking for? What capabilities do they have in-house versus outsourced? What frameworks do they use and what does their infrastructure support? What will the technical integration look like? Understanding technical patterns will feed back to your customer prioritisation (see 'Find common patterns and prioritise') and product roadmap – which customers can deploy fast and what capabilities are you missing?

Behaviour over feelings. Questionnaires like Net Promoter Score or questions such as, 'How would you feel about not being able to use the product?' put the customer in a hypothetical situation and can reflect a *falsely* positive sentiment making you feel good. Remember 'The art of asking good questions' – we care about facts as measured by customer behaviours. Customer behaviour will often indicate problems well ahead of time: Is their usage going down? Are they disengaged and failing to provide feedback, positive or negative? Is the contract nearing its end and they have still not asked to renegotiate pricing or request an extension? Have they promised to introduce you to additional internal business units, but it never happened? Have you learned that they are evaluating your competitors? Is/has your champion left the company and you have not been handed over to anyone *friendly*? Always monitor customer behaviour and learn why it changes directly from them. This includes investigating an improvement against your KPIs as well – negative feedback helps refine the product, retain existing customers or adapt your hypothesis, while positive feedback can help scale existing customer usage and acquire new customers.

If the customer has already left, the best way to learn why is to just ask. Make sure you are not burning any bridges and try to be as useful in their transition as you can. The world is small and, as we've said before, reputation is hard to build, and easy to lose. Be mindful that most of the time they will not want to (or be able to) share their actual reasons for leaving (similar to the reasoning discussed in 'Pilots that do not progress') – after all you clearly missed all the leading indicators and the customer has already made their decision. Evaluate the following:

- **Problem.** Does the customer still have the problem you identified? Has anything changed in their industry (regulation, economy, etc) or to the company itself (leadership, revenues, etc)? Why is the problem no longer a priority for them? Review in line with 'Step 2: test the problem'.

- **Solution.** Are you still solving the main customer problem correctly? Has your product, approach or value proposition changed? Do the value/unit economics still hold? Do your and the customer's KPIs align? Why is your solution not resulting in the expected ROI for the customer? Review in line with 'Step 3: test the solution'.

- **MVP.** Have you delivered the minimum capabilities that are required to show value? Have you communicated your value correctly? Have you structured and delivered against the pilot goals? Does your product have the expected performance, UX and lack of major bugs for the core functionality? Is it easy enough to onboard the customer? Has your product changed (new, removed or changed features), thus affecting the customer's (perceived) value ROI? Have you miscommunicated your product capabilities or their maturity, or was there a difference between their expectation and reality? Review in line with 'Minimum viable product (MVP)' and Chapter Nine.

- **Support.** Have you made your customer support process clear? Have you handled all customer support requests professionally and in a timely manner? Have you understood and delivered promises to their expectation? Have you made your internal champion look like a star by supplying all the materials and representing them well, even when they are not around?

- **Competition.** Has your customer found an alternative product? What won them over (e.g. price, features, performance, support, brand, commercial arrangements, internal relationships, etc)? What was the biggest issue with your product for them? How can you win them back?

ACT II

INCREASING THE BUSINESS FLYWHEEL MOMENTUM

Now you've got the basics down with the tools and frameworks of the business development flywheel, it's time to up your game, to understand the inside tips to becoming a master executor. In other words – let's start increasing the flywheel momentum.

That means everything from making new friends, to navigating your first contract to getting to grips with what product-market fit really means (hint – it's about finding the value exchange that achieves scale), to preparing for future scale and raising external funding.

The key thing to take from this part of the book – remember the introduction section on why startups fail? – is that you simply do not truly understand your customer. The massively simplified reason for why startups fail is that they just don't understand their customer enough and it's because they're missing the key fundamental: that we are all people. Let's make it very clear: customers + markets = people.

CHAPTER ELEVEN
Making new friends

...HOW TO SPEAK TO SOMEONE WHO DOES NOT EVEN
KNOW YOUR NAME

Humans are social creatures and we inherently want to be liked by our peers. As we discussed in 'The art of good questions', people will lie to you, thinking that they are doing you a favour and sometimes they will make promises that they cannot keep, too. To move from *saying* to *doing*, it requires energy (i.e. a sacrifice in the form of time, money, action, etc). Priorities and top problems change all the time and what is significant to you as a startup might be immaterial to an established enterprise. During the very early days of AimBrain, when it was just the two founders, we managed to close a paid pilot with a tier one financial institution. The pilot cost, £50,000, was the maximum that could be signed off before the procurement team needed to get involved. It was more than our salaries combined at the time. But it was worth more than money; we would get access to millions of their users to train and improve our product. It was a huge win for us. Everything was going well – we received the payment for the pilot in full and had a go-live date scheduled. Throughout there was a strong collaboration between us and our internal champion. Suddenly, we did not hear from them for a week, which was unusual. It did not set off any alarms in our heads – they'd already paid for the pilot, so it would be a huge loss for them to discontinue it before even seeing the results, right? Wrong. A week later we learned that 'internal priorities had changed' and that all resources dedicated to us were now being shifted to different projects. They did not even *try* asking for the £50,000 back. As a founder you must always be fostering new relationships while validating your leads and building relationships with existing customers.

Building and fostering relationships with people – a.k.a. the customers

Customers can be slayers or kingmakers – they'll kill off your startup before it has even begun or help to accelerate you into a stratosphere never before envisaged. Customers are logical – with numbers, revenues, challenges to solve and customers of their own to deal with – and yet equally irrational and frustrating, making decisions which baffle and seem to make no sense. Connecting with these creatures of allure and mystery is a challenging and daunting process, especially for companies and individuals who have never engaged with customers as the one key factor standing between failure and success. The greatest fact about customers is that they are *people* – they are individuals, they have families, ambitions, failures, successes, they read books, try to do their best, sometimes succeed at being awesome and generally want to make their worlds better. Connecting with customers is really all about connecting with individuals. Indeed, they operate within their own ecosystems, which are often driven by varying motives, but that does not make them any less like you or me. We have to understand their experience from their perspective within their environments.

Always be validating

Remember Step 4 of the business-development cycle: you need to cast aside past events or verbal commitments, and observe your potential customer's *current* actions. They are the leading indicators for your momentum:

- **Communication velocity.** How fast do they respond to your emails? Do they chase you if you do not respond quickly?
- **Usage metrics.** Have they completed integration or the first time setup? How often do they use your product? Are they engaged?
- **Deal momentum.** Are they sending more questions to you, than you to them? Are they following up asking for ETAs and

when it will be ready to test? Are they introducing you to new internal teams that would benefit from your solution?

- **Association**. Are they OK with you mentioning their name in press releases? Better, yet, are they sending press releases including your name themselves? Are they inviting you to participate on panels with them? Are they showcasing you in their innovation centres? Do their architecture slides, internal or otherwise, have your name/logo in relevant places?
- **Validation**. Are they confirming in writing, what has been verbally agreed? Are they happy for you to share that with potential investors? Are they OK with signing a Letter of Intent? Are they happy to have a reference call as part of an investment due diligence process? Do they sync with you before any of the reference calls?
- **Strategy.** Are they sharing their private future roadmap and priorities? Are they keen to invest in your venture?

Of course, each of these is very dependent on your specific sector and circumstances – the goal is to develop mutually beneficial relationships that extend beyond just signing a legal contract. Many times we have seen a conversation turn into a customer simply because we focused on mutual value creation rather than a short-sighted transactional interaction.

One step further, you can arrange catch-ups with your (potential) customers on a regular basis (e.g. every two weeks), to discuss how you are doing in their eyes, how you could improve, and to update them on relevant industry news or share company developments and ask for their input.

CHAPTER TWELVE
Negotiating your first contract

...AND ENTERPRISE CONTRACT GOTCHAS

Before starting any negotiation, it is crucial to know what your deal breakers are and be willing to walk away if they are not met. You simply cannot afford to work with unreasonable clients. You'll be able to tell your negotiations are going well when the client starts selling themselves to you (for example, telling you how many users or what volume they have, how fast they can deploy you, what successes they've had in the past, how much they like working with innovative companies, etc).

Make everyone win

Picture the negotiations for your first contract as a game of tennis. The legal contract is the net. Essentially, you are engaging in a value exchange across the net, which means people taking positions, firing shots and trying to score points. Unlike tennis, however, this game is only over when you both win. Aim for a mutually agreeable compromise. Expect that this will be an interchange and that it will take time to get to know each other. Your role is to understand your customer and to make decisions on what you will include in the value exchange. There will be lots of different opinions on what you should and shouldn't do. Get input from legal, get insight from your technical and commercial teams – it will never be perfect, but ultimately you need to take ownership of the final call. Making everyone feel like a winner is a bit like flirting – you need to make it happen without being too obvious or direct about your intentions.

Remember, while the well executed tennis exchange is a crucial prerequisite to your long-term customer relationship, the result, i.e. the contract, is almost never referred to again. Think about it as risk management, because if you or your customer ever needs to cite any specifics of it, your relationship is almost certainly *not* going well.

Value intellectual property

Intellectual property (IP) is the most important part of the contract. You must get it right from the very first legal interaction. This could easily be the difference between your company having a significant exit and not being able to raise any external funding. To get it right, you must have all the rights and ownership to all IP generated or derived as part of the engagement. Do not try to negotiate this part yourself – this is one of the areas where you want to have competent contract lawyers helping you.

Keep a record of IP ownership for all engagements. Never delay for a later date or event. Always mutually sign it as part of an NDA, pilot agreement or commercial agreement, before *any* work is done, even if you are under deadline pressure. Explain to any hesitant customers that in order to deliver value today and in the future, your company needs to own the IP because of future fundraising (redirect any negativity from yourself to your shareholders or the company board). And crucially, be willing to walk away if your customer is not on the same page.

Customers might also ask for exclusivity. It makes sense for them – if your product delivers the value it promises, they want to be the first (and only) ones in the market capturing it for as long as they can. Generally, do not agree to any exclusivity, no matter what promises the customer is making. Only consider it in extreme situations, for example, if you are running out of money and have an offer on the table for two years subscription with an upfront lump sum payment for exclusivity in a region you are not likely to focus on much for the next two years. Exclusivity will slow down your growth and stop the build › measure › learn cycle. If the situation arises, explain that it is actually in their own best interests for you to learn from other companies – it will help improve the product and, as a result, their ROI without any additional cost to them. Again, be willing to walk away if they are not on the same page.

Make sure to pay the same level of attention to IP with employees, interns, consultants, third parties, advisors and yourselves, the founding team.[30]

Deliberately design contract length

Just like with pilot agreements (see 'Pilot-to-production agreement'), never ever sign no-clear-start or no-clear-end contracts. If customers are not willing to progress from the evaluation phase, find out why and be willing to terminate the service if they refuse to move on this. Relationships need to be mutually beneficial and you are creating value for them at your own cost without anything in return.

As you scale the company, different commercial proof points will be important for you and your external stakeholders:

1. At the early stage, your focus is on demonstrating product-market fit with innovators and early adopters (see 'What's the difference between business development and sales?'). At this point, you won't know all the market details or have an exact scalable sales model. Your focus should be on retaining your customers while you iron out all the kinks and inevitably make mistakes. At this early stage, aim for contract lengths to be on the longer side – one year to one year and a half. Longer contract terms will act as a buffer while you get your business in order so that you can demonstrate the market product need and your commercial capabilities.

2. Once you have proven the product-market fit, your goal is to prove that you can indeed scale the sales process with the early and late majority. You should have a relatively stable product and you are less likely to pivot your business model. You have well-defined customer personas and you are aiming to capture the majority of the market. At this stage, aim for contracts to be on the short-to-medium side – three to six months. Medium contract length will allow you to iterate the build › measure ›

learn cycle much faster, adapting to new learning or changing market conditions, including events from competition and your own findings. Low churn with short contracts will serve as an undeniable measure of market success. In other words, you have proven that customers are staying with you not because of a contractual lock-in, but because they continue to receive value from your product and that your brand is preferred over your competitors in that specific vertical.

3. Once you have proven that your sales process scales, and have captured the majority of the market, you will want to focus on the laggards. At this stage you have a very stable product with low churn and a list of references. It is likely a commoditised market now and you are looking to expand into new markets or verticals. Laggards usually require significant sales effort and time, simply because of their size and procurement requirements. Your results need to reflect that. Aim for long-term contracts of two or more years. This will also act as a buffer in terms of revenue while you define, test and scale any new offerings or expand to new verticals.

Appreciate that customers will have their own preferences and biases. For example, some might have a rule that they only sign minimum one-year contracts. Some might also see short contracts as a risk for your product support or a sign that you are looking to exit, and go with your competitors instead, who can offer them the reassurance of a two-plus years contract. It will be very specific to your industry, product and market adoption stage. Do not shoot yourself in the foot trying to prove low churn with short contracts – having customers is still a priority. And *always* validate your assumptions with them first!

Continuously validate the pricing

Base your pricing for the next 12 to 18 months on your value exchange with the first few customers. Double-check your insights with the customer directly by asking what their expectations are for cost and why. From this you will learn about standard market margins and be able to update your Lean Canvas model. Your pricing will evolve over time and will change as you get to know your customers better. Think about your pricing mechanism:

- Per active end-user?
- Per internal user or employee?
- License per instance, region or channel?
- Per each transaction, API call or volume by buckets?
- Flat monthly or yearly subscription?
- Tiered pricing structure based on functionality?

The rule of thumb is to target your price point to generate an ROI ratio[31] of four to nine for the customer. Another way of looking at it is to aim to capture 10% to 20% of the value that you create. When defining 'value', account beyond the obvious tangible sources:

- How much would it cost your customers to replicate this in-house in terms of engineering and management time, recruitment fees, advisory fees, admin fees, etc? Similarly, how long would it take for them to fill those positions?
- If they decide to build this, what are they not building (opportunity cost)?
- How much have they already invested in solving this problem (e.g. trying to build it themselves or sourcing vendors)?
- How much revenue are they losing each day without your product?
- How much value, new revenue and brand recognition will they get as early adopters?

Generally, the earlier you are in the market-adoption cycle, the higher ROI you want your customers to have from your product. Your pricing mechanism must be aligned with your customer's goals or KPIs and grow with usage, otherwise you will end up losing money.

Also consider that different customer segments will look at and measure value differently, requiring different pricing levels and potentially even strategies, which is not a problem at this stage (see 'Find common patterns and prioritise'). Make your pricing easy to understand and outline all assumptions explicitly, in line with your customer's own projections. If you cannot demonstrate at least five times *quantifiable* return for the customer, it is very unlikely that they will adopt your product.

Don't worry about getting the pricing exactly right – your primary goal now is to achieve product-market fit. If all else fails and you are completely lost, specifically on pricing, either pick an amount you think is reasonable from your market insights or ask your potential customers what they would be willing to pay. The goal here is to be decisive and learn as fast as you can, rather than procrastinate on trying to find the perfect number.

Finding the *right* price is a process. With each new customer and contract renewal, keep raising your price until 20% of your customers do not convert or churn because of it – that is your rough ballpark figure for optimal price. Mathematically you want to maximise the product of unit price and customer volume, but real-life is rarely an elegant equation, requiring many iterations to find what works best. If you consistently lose customers because of your price, check your market pricing assumptions. As with everything, the detail is in the execution. If you raise prices for your existing customers without being able to clearly justify a higher value (e.g. a more stable product, better support, new features – i.e. reframing your current product as more premium and mature than when you started),[32] it will leave a negative impression of your brand. Do not give your competitors the opportunity to out-execute you. Losing only a few customers to optimise your overall revenue is part of the process, losing a market – game over.

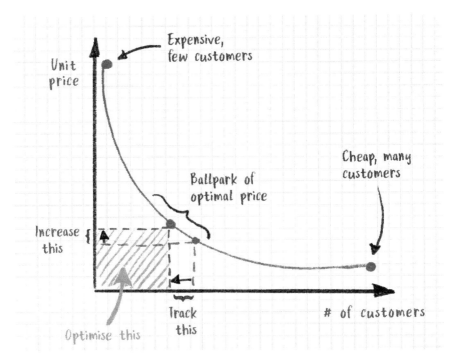

Hypothetical product demand curve. As the price goes up, the demand goes down and inversely. Increase the price and track customer churn to maximise your revenue.

Revenue aside, higher price means fewer customers, which means lower operational and support overheads and thus better focus and faster iterations. You can always lower the price at a later stage, but there is a limit to how many customers you are realistically able to support in these early days. Customers who are willing to pay the higher price are usually the ones who *really* have the problem you are solving, thus, self-selecting themselves as your target audience. However, do not use the opposite as a convenient excuse when a customer leaves: 'Oh, they just weren't our target market!'

Just as with precisely defining start and end dates of a contract, never sign one without a minimum payment commitment from your customer (i.e. the minimum they are expected to pay for ongoing service maintenance irrespective of their usage – even if usage is zero). At

AimBrain we sometimes found ourselves in situations where we spent significant amounts of time on commercial contracts (also take into account all the energy it took to get to that stage of the sales process), only for those companies to sign and simply never implement our product (for whatever reason). If your customer is not willing to agree to a minimum commitment, really review if you have the validation and buy-in that you think you do. Explain that your shareholders or the board are really strict on company priorities and that the minimum commitment is to partially cover the operating costs and is insignificant compared to their usage projections.

No matter the size of your customer, they will ask for, and usually expect, a discount, so build that into your pricing strategy. Understand if the discount request is 'make it or break it' (e.g. there is no further budget) or 'nice to have' (e.g. your champion wants to look good in front of procurement). For the former, even if the customer absolutely loves your product, you need to evaluate if it is a one-off situation or a wider trend. If it is a wider trend, find a market or a problem with a target audience that is not fully commoditised and has money, or adjust your hypothesis. For the latter, you need to understand exactly who is asking for a discount and why. Recognise who initiated the discount conversation – sometimes it means you're speaking with a procurement person – but concentrate on the person with the problem you're solving and the budget holder (these may be the same or different people). Remember, it is like a game of tennis (see Chapter Eleven): address their core concerns reasonably without giving in on everything they ask for. If it is because they are early adopters or your product is unproven, explain that you giving a discount will not address those concerns. In fact, higher pricing will allow you to support them better. If it is because they feel like you need them to enable/accelerate the development of your product that you will later make available for everyone, including their competitors, explain that the proposed pricing is already very aggressive and reflects the nature of the early collaborative relationship (i.e. you will naturally cater to early client needs more than to the later ones). If there is still any pushback, explain that it would be a shame to lose a customer purely on pricing, but you need to prioritise your time with other clients. Offer to meet them in the middle – propose a discount if they sign a multi-year contract, offset the discount amount by increasing the minimum commitment, create volume or tier-based pricing, offer to include a set amount of additional support for the first year or include already existing product capabilities outside of their plan (e.g. advanced reporting), etc. Also ask *them* to be creative and suggest a suitable arrangement that would not be via a direct cash discount. Explain that showing strong numbers is important to get your shareholder(s) and the board to sign off this agreement.

From our experience, the best commercial relationships are never about pricing, but about value creation and fair reward with the expectation to have it reinvested back into the product and customer support. If the customer really has the problem you are solving, they will focus on testing your solution as fast as possible, rather than worrying about anyone else. If they do genuinely worry about their competition or see you very strategic to their roadmap, that would usually result in an acquisition offer.

Nail the references and due diligence

If the problem is painful enough for your customer, references rarely come up as a talking point. They should understand your company's level of maturity and be focused on the solution rather than your commercial progress validation. Your pilot results *are* the best reference. That being said, when references do come up, they are often a legal checkbox exercise. In this case, negotiate with the customer that any referencing will be done only after the legal contract is fully defined and agreed by both parties in principle, and – if you can get away with it – signed. Explain that you are happy to provide as many references as they see fit, but it would be unfair to use your referees' time unless you are absolutely sure that the contract will be executed. The same applies the other way – you would not be asking for references from all the potential prospects, only the really serious ones.

Another due diligence point that comes up frequently is around your financial viability. No one wants to spend energy on integration and then start looking for a new vendor in a year, if you go out of business. To address that, the customer will likely ask for financial statements – do not share them. As a startup you *do not* have viable financials and anything that you share can only be used against you. Remember, people talk, and that information might end up with your competitors. You going out of business is, frankly, a legitimate worry and sharing financial information will not solve that, but you getting more customers will. If you already have investors, offer to arrange a reference call between them and the customer to reassure them that your company is doing well and that the investors will continue to financially support you. If the customer is still asking for financials, explain that as a private company you are not allowed to share financials by the board. You could offer to place your software/code/documentation in a third-party software escrow, paid for by the customer (since they asked for it), to address any remaining concerns. On top of that, you can also suggest that in case you do go out of business, your support staff will be available for one to three months (aligned with your employment agreement notice period) on a consulting basis, paid for by the customer. It's a win-win situation – the customer gets reassurance that the service will not just stop abruptly one day and your staff will have a financial buffer for transition in the worst-case scenario of you ceasing to trade.

Refine the service-level agreement

If your product or service is deemed business-critical, the customer will expect a service-level agreement (SLA). Key points to think about:

Uptime. Define precisely what is the expected service uptime and how you will measure it. Depending on your criticality – for example, are you a service that a single internal employee uses from time to time? Or are you a service that online banking relies on to the extent that your downtime means no customer can login to the portal? – expect to be asked for between 99% and 99.9% uptime. To allow yourself more breathing room each time a catastrophic failure happens (and it will) ask for uptime to be measured on a yearly basis, but be ready to accept quarterly or even monthly periods. Be mindful to not come across as if your product is a risk or too immature – find out your customer expectations first.

There is a big technical difference, and thus legal implication for you, on how your product uptime is measured – for example, is it defined as an endpoint responding to a network ping, or as an API returning results within a defined strict range of outcomes? Make sure you are clear on these factors when drafting your agreement.

Sometimes customers will have unrealistic expectations for uptime, for example asking for 'five nines', i.e. 99.999%, meaning that the maximum your service can be down per year is five minutes and 15 seconds. We cannot blame them for wanting this because they may have taken that from other vendors' promises. We have seen examples of companies claiming 100% uptime and then getting creative with the commercial side of things, for example, the 100% uptime guarantee only comes after 30 minutes of downtime each month (working out at 99.93% uptime equivalent). Explain to the customer that you are happy to support higher uptime requirements, but that you will need to account for it with a higher price, since you will need to dedicate more resources just to their account. Do the math – what was your uptime historically? Which way is it trending? Assume that you will have downtime, therefore the price increase needs to cover it in full (for example, increase price to the amount of credits that you would be expected to issue based on your historical uptime performance). It is OK to promise just a bit outside of your comfort zone – it sets higher expectations for everyone. However, be mindful that you *will* have bugs and you *will* have downtime, otherwise you have likely already over-engineered the solution.[33]

When calculating downtime, make sure to only include what is within your control – network issues, cloud provider issues or third-party vendor issues do not count towards your downtime figure. Limit the scope: is the uptime calculated for your website, back office, dashboard, analyst reports or core service APIs and functions only? Is it for worldwide or the US, EMEA, etc region only?

Performance. Similar to uptime, customers will expect performance guarantees too. Essentially, how fast do you commit to processing their requests, including those with humans in the loop? Just as with uptime, make sure that anything out of your full control, like network latency or ticketing software downtime, is not part of your own performance calculation. Measure your performance in median time or percentile,[34] rather than mean (average) because you will always have some abnormal cases that take exceptionally long and would skew your statistics otherwise.

Support. Stick with three levels: service is inoperable; service is degraded; and service is affected, but correctable by documentation or future release. Define what each level means specifically for your product. Automate your ticket submission acknowledgements to meet ticket acknowledgement response deadlines, usually measured in minutes.

Maintenance. Ensure that scheduled maintenance does not count towards your downtime. Specify a reasonable notice period, usually one month, for scheduled maintenance and three to six months notice for version upgrades. Reserve the right to carry out urgent or security related maintenance with just 24 hours notice, as part of your scheduled maintenance definition.

Liability. Do not agree to any financial liability as part of the SLA, only to capped service credits or partial refund. Confirm that the SLA does not have any provisions for contract termination either. Consider if including SLA reviews (e.g. every six months) would be beneficial – it will allow you to bring all SLAs in sync or modify them based on your customer and operations experience. As an industry practice, you should not do automated refunds for downtime, but you should expect to go above and beyond the minimum contractual agreement if a customer is particularly upset with you.

Operations. If there is an outage, communicate it as soon as possible – ideally before any of the customers raise the issue themselves. Keep all affected customers in the loop on what is happening and how you are addressing the issue. If the ETA for a fix is not clear, it is best to leave it out of your communications. You don't want to set expectations and not meet them. From our experience, letting customers know that there is an issue before they realise it, and how you are addressing it, builds trust over time, and instead of becoming frustrated with you, they become your supporters during the incident. Customers understand that shit happens – it is about how fast you react and how well you keep them updated throughout.

It is best if whoever is not contributing towards an actual fix to withhold their questions, expectations and emotions. Managers or commercial people asking 'when will it be done?' only slows down the process. Never blame the team – they did the best they could in dealing with the issue. It is impossible to predict all edge scenarios. If you think that the team is underperforming, then the issue is with team management or company processes.

If the incident was long, or affected many customers, aim to send a 'Letter from the CEO' explaining what happened, why, how you addressed it and how you will make sure it does not happen again. Communication is key in building trust in your brand.

Always debrief with your team constructively and make sure to put processes in place to prevent similar outages in the future. As you cannot ever prevent all outages (e.g. even Google and Microsoft experience service downtime) cultural focus should be on processes and learning for when they do happen.

Other points to consider

Assumptions. As part of the contract, make sure to specify any assumptions (e.g. regions, channels, use-cases, teams, etc) and projections (e.g. growth) that you have received from the customer. This will ensure that all parties are on the same page and it will leave a paper trail to use as a basis for certain decisions (e.g. volume pricing).

Obligations. Note any obligations that fall on you, like industry or security certifications, and make sure you will be able to meet them – or negotiate them out of the contract. From our experience, the rule of thumb is if, based on your projections, you would *just* make it before the deadline, then do not commit. Unexpected delays, even if caused by the customer themself, mean you will definitely miss it and that will create negative energy in the relationship. Likewise, explicitly specify all of your requirements for the customer, like a dedicated integration team or a specific software stack/environment. Not meeting any of the obligations that you sign on creates an easy way out of the contract. Everyone is friendly until their budgets get tight and they start looking for opportunities to renegotiate on your price.

Timelines. Ask about the procurement process and timelines in detail as early as you can – if your champion does not know it, take it as a warning. It could be that you are the first vendor your champion is intending to buy from or, worse, that there is actually no intention to buy from you beyond the pilot. Validate. Expect the first invoice to take three months, on average, to come through. Understand who your stakeholders are – your champion, business unit, product, technical, legal and procurement teams, etc. Make sure to build rapport with each and understand what you can do to make their life easier (and hence bring about your goal faster!).

References and press releases. You *need* references from your existing customers, whereas press releases are nice to have. Ask for both, but prioritise accordingly.

Change of ownership. Irrespective of what your and your investors' strategy is today, everything has a price and you might receive an exceptional acquisition offer that makes all your shareholders very happy. Therefore, it is important to build a Change of Ownership mechanism into all your contracts – you do not want to be in a position where your company's future can be decided by a single customer. Consult with your lawyers on how that works.

CHAPTER THIRTEEN
Choosing the right market

You might already have your first customers using your product happily, but how many customers are out there in total? How big is the opportunity overall? Understanding the big-picture market opportunity is extremely important – loss-making companies with solid teams in huge markets often get VC funded over profit-generating companies with product-market fit in small markets. It makes sense in the VC equation; the majority of VC funds spread their risk by investing in multiple companies that have the *potential* of returning their *whole* fund and more (i.e. 100x+ multiple). Remember 'Competitors are just another tool' – the smaller the market, the fewer opportunities to differentiate and ultimately the less value you can capture. Irrespective of your goal – a high-growth startup or a self-sustained lifestyle or bootstrapped business – market sizing rules are universal and will be part of your growth strategy. As it is said, building a wrong product in the right market is many times better than building a right product in the wrong market. Do not fight the market, it always wins.[35] Just like with the Lean Canvas model, understanding your market is a process, so keep the market model and assumptions updated as you go along.

To put it simply, market size is an estimate of how much money is or will be spent (i.e. revenue generated) in that industry over a specific period of time (usually a year) by the businesses and consumers. It is only a tiny part of the story. Analyse the following to gauge how fertile the market is:

- Is the market commoditised (where products are differentiated mainly on price alone)?
- Do your competitors have high margins?
- What is causing the market to expand *today* (new customers, revenue growth or something else)?
- How fast has the market expanded historically?
- At what stage of growth is the market (is expansion still

accelerating, steady or already slowing down)?

- Do your competitors' growth metrics (overall revenue, web traffic, signups etc) match the historical market trends? If not, why? What other markets are they focused on?
- How many other VC-funded companies are there in the space?
- How easy is it to acquire customers?

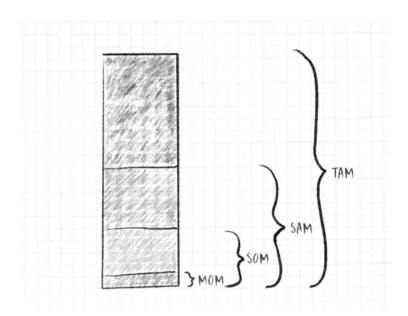

Think about your market in terms of TAM (total available market), SAM (serviceable addressable market), SOM (serviceable obtainable market) and MOM (MVP obtainable market). You might see slightly different words used for specific acronyms, but it is the concept that's important:

- **TAM.** Total available market. This is the total market (i.e. all the customers) that you *could* address with your product or service under the best-possible conditions, ignoring geographical or cultural barriers, competitors, logistical issues, local regulations, finite resources, sales models, etc. This shows the growth potential and is the answer to the eternal 'How big is your market?' question, hence the 'available' part. While it is almost impossible to reach 100% of your TAM, it is important to know this figure because it shows your vision, sets future direction and allows potential stakeholders (investors, employees and yourself) to quickly judge the opportunity. Each new product has its own total available market. The TAM assumes a full market adoption by everyone, from innovators to laggards. Taking AimBrain as an example, our TAM was biometric identity as a service that could be used by anyone for online access, ID schemes (e.g. government, healthcare or transportation), remote onboarding, authentication, verification, liveliness proofing, etc.

- **SAM**. Serviceable addressable market. This is the portion of TAM that you can realistically address, taking into account your current reach (geographical, cultural, legal, product limitations, etc) and unit metrics, such as your product's lifetime value (LTV), customer acquisition cost (CAC), etc, hence the 'addressable' part. As you scale into new regions or verticals, each will be defined as a new SAM within the same TAM. This should represent your goals for the next two to three years. In terms of market adoption, this includes everyone from innovators to early majority. In terms of customers to prioritise, this includes everyone from the proactive, reactive and on hold groups. Success in the SAM bracket will be proof of a scalable sales process for later stage investors (Series B+). SAM is usually the answer to 'What is your next market?' question. To be considered as doing exceptionally well, aim to capture 5%–10% of your SAM. Continuing AimBrain's example, our SAM was financial institutions in the EMEA.

- **SOM**. Serviceable obtainable market. This is the portion of SAM that you are focused on obtaining within the next eight to eighteen months, hence the 'obtainable' part. This bracket is second in importance to MOM and is the answer to the 'What is your target market?' question. You should take into account your current team and hiring plans, company and product capabilities, competition and available funding or resources. This is the place to focus on reality, rather than aspirations. Your next significant funding round (late seed or Series A) will depend on demonstrable SOM success. In terms of adoption, this includes innovators and early adopters. In terms of customers to prioritise, these should be everyone from the proactive and reactive groups. With our AimBrain example, our SOM was behavioural biometric authentication for Financial Institutions in the UK that either had a significant amount of fraud due to stolen credentials in their mobile or online channels, or wanted to use behavioural biometrics as part of two-factor authentication (looking back, the latter was a distraction that we wasted too much time on).

- **MOM**. MVP obtainable market. The smallest, but most important part. This is the portion of your SOM on which you should focus your current and immediate progress over the next six months. It includes your current customers and everyone that can be onboarded with your existing MVP without any significant changes. This group should be discussed with your team on a weekly basis, at least. Success here will drive your immediate funding. These are your market innovators and customers from the proactive group. MOM is the answer to 'Who are your current customers?' question.

- **PAN.** Potential Available Market. This is your grandiose vision, an absolute nirvana state. We left this one out for a reason: while good for getting people excited, PAN is not useful in actually bringing you closer to it. Returning to AimBrain's example, our PAN was 'identity'. Identity of people (online, physical access, biometrics, implants, government IDs, self-sovereign IDs, etc) and of things (smart devices, autonomous entities, etc). While PAN should be part of your pitch to show grandiose ambition, it is best left out of any calculations.

There are two main methods for sizing your market:

- **Top-down.** As the name suggests, you begin at the very top, a TAM estimate, and then apply filters to narrow it down at each stage to your target market, SOM. Be brutally honest with your assumptions and be able to defend your numbers in detail. It is much better to over-restrict than be the person who presents SOM like this: 'TAM is 100 billion, so if we only capture 0.1% of the market (and assume a standard 10x multiple on revenue for a SaaS business), that makes us a billion-dollar company.' It makes you look naive.

- **Bottom-up.** Here you need to break down what you know from your customers, based on their metrics and projections, and then scale it up to the total market. Think about how much a single customer pays (MOM or competitor pricing), how many customers your can realistically obtain (SOM), how many customers you can address within your reach (SAM) and how many customers there could be in total, assuming no limitations (TAM) and how all of that that changes over time.

Bottom-up is our preferred method as you are working with facts, rather than assumptions. It forces you to interact with potential customers and sounds credible when presented to external stakeholders. However, it is a good idea to use both methods for a sanity check – your estimated numbers should be within the same order of magnitude. If they are not, revisit your assumptions by talking to sources of information directly (customers, analysts, VCs, etc) or use the smaller number. One could argue that top-down works only with established markets and therefore you can only estimate the market bottom-up if you are *creating* it. But as we covered in our previous chapters – in most cases you simply cannot *afford* to create or define a new market.

Keep your market estimation process simple and start with:

- **Analyst reports, VC themed pieces (as they usually try to explain how big the market is to back up their investment decisions), Google Adwords, Medium, Twitter, Reddit and other social sites to gather market insights, as well as reaching out to your potential customers.** Ensure you double-check sources and understand exactly what is and is not included in the figure. Reach out to your sources directly if you find contradicting information – it can often lead to a good discussion that helps further validate your assumptions or provides non-obvious market insights. Take note who the market influencers are – you will want to have good relationships with them.

- **LinkedIn is a goldmine for customer data.** Everyone has volunteered their information. It helps break down why your customers' roles and personas of your customers exist and it provides an insight into your connections, plus how big their companies are. Also take note of the groups that specific people are part of, and what marketing channels they use – often you will find more target customers there.

- **Customers – especially the publicly traded/held ones.** Use their company reports, which are usually available to the public via their shareholder knowledge portals, to uncover insights and figures relevant to what you are looking for. This is one of the most overlooked resources; sometimes, you can seem incredibly knowledgeable to a potential customer because you managed to read *their* key customer's shareholder report. So find relevant individuals (the ones who fit your buying personas) and follow them on public channels. Often they will share market insights and you will learn what makes them tick. You should know your early customers deep in their organisations, how they're evaluated, what success looks like for the organisation and the rationale behind it.

- **Competitors.** Read their reports, case studies, blogs and social media. This will often include some market research. Learn what groups, forums or alliances they are part of and see if you can join any sessions as an observer (without paying!).

Market sizing is not about being right in your revenue or market-share numbers, it is a process to clarify and write down your assumptions, align your team, inform your roadmap focus and to have a sanity check, before you spend huge amounts of the only thing that you cannot get more of in life – time. As a rule of thumb, if you are after VC-fuelled growth, your TAM should be more than $1 billion with a path to $100 million annual recurring revenue (ARR) for them to be even slightly interested. Think about it – some of the funds themselves manage more than $100 million in assets.

Finally, market-share control is a constant race; the early majority tend to buy from the category leader[36] – make sure it is you. Remember, it is not the first to the market who wins, but the first to product-market fit. So move fast, keeping your focus on making as few mistakes as you can, rather than on being right. Keep SAM in your crosshairs at all times, while nailing MOM and SOM execution.

CHAPTER FOURTEEN
What the hell is product-market fit, anyway?

Product-market fit (PMF) is a *process* rather than an event – you cannot just 'achieve it' and be done with it. You need to be constantly improving it. It is also not a well defined linear path; you need to always be observing the market and adjusting to its new priorities. As we've said before (and will repeat endlessly), it is not the first to the market, but first to PMF that wins. To generalise, PMF is a continuous process of uncovering problems (the 'market' bit), creating solutions to them (the 'product' bit) and measuring how much value someone gets because of it (the 'fit' bit), in that order. Much easier said than done. While your goal right now is to validate your hypothesis, you do need to start putting the right processes in place to set yourself for success.

Again, there is no one-size-fits-all definition[37] of what PMF is – it is more of an art than a science, a matter of combining all the different tools. It is a skill that you will hone as a founder. Think about PMF as a physics resonant frequency[38] – you are not exactly sure where it is (because real-life systems are often too complex to have exact systems), but you can measure it and identify when you are going in the right direction, and once you are in the ballpark, even if not exactly spot on, the system will amplify its own signal.

You will often need to make the hard decision about whether to stay your course or change direction. You will never have a full view or the perfect team (see ACT III), so always be on the lookout for some leading indicators that your current approach is not working:
- If you are having a lot of conversations with potential customers, responding to RFPs (requests for proposal), and even having paid pilots, but they are not *converting* to a purchase. This problem is especially dangerous for early founders, we ourselves made the mistake of relying on pilots as a problem-

solution validation. But we learned that we should have treated it just like a *small part* of our conversion funnel as opposed to its main objective. It is relatively cheap for a large corporation to run a pilot and therefore you need to validate that they are looking to *buy* rather than to *learn* from you (see Chapter Nine and 'Always be validating').

- Similarly, if you are talking to a lot of 'innovation' or 'change' teams, or are trialled in internal 'labs' or 'sandboxes' as opposed to production environments. As we discussed in previous sections (see 'Be wary of innovation teams'), these teams rarely have any purchasing power and their KPIs are usually different to company priorities. If you get directed to them by the business units, re-evaluate your buying personas because these companies clearly do not have, or recognise, the problem that you are solving.

- If you find yourself *pushing* the problem, rather than getting *pulled* for the solution, it's another bad sign. You get introduced to more and more teams internally who are keen to listen to your pitch, but are not in any hurry to buy. Instead of the account progressing through the sales funnel, each stage gets bigger and takes longer. Conversations revolve more around market trends, your approach and differentiation, than about their problem and how they can capture the value from your product. Another telltale sign is that you talk more than you get to listen during the meetings. Re-evaluate and requalify the priority (maybe move them from proactive or reactive) and be willing to walk away from the opportunity.

- If your churn is growing with new customers. As you learn more about the market and customer segment, the more focused your product and target market become, and thus churn should go down. If your churn is increasing, it is like a bucket with holes – sure, you can fill it up for a moment, but it will drain and be useless without a constant refilling effort. Re-evaluate your MVP and target market – have you built the *right* solution? Are you communicating it well? Is there a different customer segment for whom the problem is a bigger priority?

It is to be expected that you will have a few or even many iterations of the build › measure › learn cycle until you nail the PMF. What you must avoid, though, are vanity metrics – measuring something that makes you feel good, but does not actually bring you any closer to the goal:

- **Funding stage is not reflective of the PMF.** Many companies fundraise based on their runaway (or lack of it) rather than actual progress – you need to meet milestones and then take funding to meet further milestones, rather than treat funding as a milestone on its own. It is easy to drink your own kool-aid and convince yourself that you are making progress each time you close a new round – it excites employees and the press, after all. The truth is, you can always find more capital, but taking on more funding without meeting significant milestones puts you on borrowed time. It is unlikely that you will ever catch up.

- **Company valuation is in no way proof of your market fit either.** It feels good to have a high company valuation – you must be doing something right! The truth is that early on, valuation is a number that reflects how excited you can make potential investors. Real valuation will hit you like a brick wall once it is time to exit – public shareholders and acquirers will set your value based on measurable progress, rather than vision.

- **Sentiment, like a Net Promoter Score (NPS), is not an indicator for PMF.** Customers will often want to make you feel good, as it is part of human nature to avoid confrontation. They will say that everything is great, while already looking for an alternative behind your back (see 'The art of good questions'). Net Promoter Score reflects intention, but you should focus on action – asking how likely someone would be to recommend a product is a hypothetical question. On the other hand, actually *measuring* how many people have shared or recommended your product and *learning* why (and why not) is very powerful and will steer you in the right direction.

- **Revenue that is not from your core product does not count here.** It is great to get paid for pilots. It is also part of the early journey to have a significant proportion of revenue from professional services. However, that does not scale well at later market adoption stages, so focus on repeatable revenue, although even then it is a lagging indicator.

- **Other metrics that are not reflective of your PMF.** Sales team headcount if you hired them to 'get more sales' as opposed to 'not being able to handle inbound customer demand', number of commercial partners, size of leadership team, experience and talent within the team, number of features in the product, number of press mentions, number of entries in your mailing list (unless that is your actual business/ product!)… the list can go on.

To know if you are heading in the right direction early, focus on the customer behaviour. You want:

- **Growing active customers.** Define what 'active' is in your specific context – make sure that the metric is aligned with the value mechanism and will scale with the delivered value amount (hint: the number of signed contracts or customer logins does not matter, whereas value delivery events, such as your product evaluation with their data or test deployments in their environment do). What a good usage benchmark looks like will very much depend on your industry, but you should have a good feel for it from your customer interview sessions. Track customer cohorts each time you have a new hypothesis iteration. Understand exactly *what* delivers the most value to the customer and *how* the customers consume it. Growing your active customers indicates that you have found the right problem.

- **Growing customer activity.** Growing your active customers is just part of the story. You might be adding new customers only for them to never come back after their first experience with your product, either because it lacks the minimum functionality to deliver value, or their expectations were not met. Work with your customers to understand what growth they expect – specifically in the context of your product – and compare it against their actual usage over time. If it does not match, understand *why* and act on it. Growth here indicates that you found the right solution for the problem and increases your customer lifetime value (LTV).

- **Growing referrals.** Finally, your customers might sometimes be forced to use your product, either for political reasons, contract lock-in or lack of alternatives, but would replace you at the first opportunity, so clearly, they would not recommend you to their peers. This is why it is important to also track your customer referrals. Simply ask any existing customers if they have referred you to anyone, internally or otherwise. If they have not, understand *why* and *what* it would take for them to do so. Likewise, ask any new customers how they heard about you. Understand how many days it takes for a new customer to refer you and what is the exact trigger event – because you will want to scale that. Word of mouth referrals indicate that you found the right target market for the solution and lowers your customer acquisition cost (CAC).

Once you find a repeatable sales model and start scaling, you should also be obsessed with the following:

- **Increasing the LTV:CAC ratio.** While this is a later-stage indicator and only meaningful after you already have a number of customers, it is arguably the most important metric to track. Simply put, it predicts how scalable your sales model is. As rule of thumb, for it to be a viable model, your LTV should be three times larger than the CAC (i.e. LTV > CAC×3). While measuring LTV, assume the worst outcome – that customers will terminate at the end of their contract period. Do the same for CAC: take into account your sales bonus, software tools cost, sales travel and other expenses too. The ratio will inform your margins and thus sales strategy, pricing, channels and marketing focus. As a sanity check, aim for your customers to become profitable to you by year two.[39]
- **Decreasing customer and revenue churn**. While a lagging indicator, customer and revenue churn acts as one of the primary sanity checks for validating the end-to-end business processes (i.e. pricing, value delivery, customer support, ongoing product differentiation, etc). Any time your customer leaves, understand *why* it happened and observe repeating patterns – those are your focus areas to fix. In general, it will cost you five times more to acquire a new customer than to retain an existing one. Increasing churn can indicate your lack of focus, new competitive entrants and strategies or changing market priorities – this is why PMF is a process rather than an event. It is important to track both revenue and customer churn. Consider a situation where you track only revenue churn: say you are losing customers to competitors, but the remaining customers deliver expansion revenue over the lost revenue and thus mask the overall issue. Also consider where you only track customer churn: if your biggest account leaves that would track as just one customer. This might be offset by onboarding new accounts, but that single company leaving might mean a 50% reduction in your revenue.

- **Net negative revenue churn**. This is another lagging indicator, which also takes into account existing customers from who you've seen an expansion in revenue. A net negative revenue churn is when your additional revenue growth from *existing* customers outweighs the revenue that you lose from customers leaving or downgrading. Additional revenue growth usually comes from upsales (more of the same product with the same buyer) and cross-sales (different product with the same buyer). Having a net negative revenue churn proves that you have a built-in growth and value capture mechanism part of your product and that you no longer solely rely on new customer acquisition to grow. As a rule of thumb, aim for approximately -2% net MRR churn rate[40] to scale exponentially. (Note the difference between net and gross revenue churn – the latter does not take revenue expansion into account.)[41]

Customer behaviour matters above intention, and is measurable even before you have launched the specific item or a feature. Pre-orders, signups to a paid priority product release queue, product functions that are 'in development' and only available as a prepaid add-on, or items that can be purchased on 'back-order' – are all measurable events that ask something *meaningful* from the customer and are strong indicators of interest. In case you decide not to proceed, simply return the money and explain that based on market interest it would not be a viable approach.

There is no magic number to tell you what 'good' looks like in each of the metrics above – they are very dependent on your specific circumstances and should be informed by your customers or industry and growth plans. It is up to you to know the market averages and set milestones for your company that will put you well above it. As a guideline, if at later stages (Series A+) you demonstrate a *consistent* and *sustained* 20% month-on-month growth of your main KPI, you are in a very strong position – perhaps even exponential growth.[42] One exception: if you are taking on VC money, aim to increase your valuation 100x over eight years (for SaaS assume 10x multiple on revenue), and then work backwards on what each component's graph needs to be.

The product will end up speaking for you, hopefully on a daily basis. Getting PMF metrics right as a seed-based startup will require deep customer insight, often some work 'consulting' with customers and most definitely several iterations of your pricing model. The stronger your PMF is, the harder it is to unseat you, even with a cheaper or superior product – suddenly your customers are themselves amplifying your sales and the business flywheel accelerates at a compounding pace. If you get this right, you can get almost everything else early wrong (culture, product, hiring, fundraising, commercials, etc) and still win. As a rule, for a B2B business you need to achieve PMF within the first 18 to 24 months of your company's formation, otherwise you will likely run out of money or motivation.

To sum it up, product-market fit is the ongoing process of your product solving customer problems and your business growing as a consequence of that. Only at that point you can scale the business sustainably.

CHAPTER FIFTEEN
Raising your first round

If your business flywheel is accelerating at an increasing rate, and you already have a significant sales pipeline at various stages, you will likely want to raise funds even before your tenth customer to make sure that you are able to keep that momentum going. But *really* consider if you want to take outside money to grow – if you do, have appreciation for what you are getting yourself, your team, friends and family into. Investments are for accelerating your company growth – creating a higher return in absolute terms where everyone wins, not for exploring your hobbies or pausing business activities when you feel like it. Only raise money if your ultimate goal is global domination because once you get on the treadmill, you are committed to running.

Just as with your own goals, the proof points investors will look for will change with the maturity of your company. As we discussed before, your funding stage might not be representative of your company's progress (see Chapter Fourteen), however, be mindful that by using certain industry terms, like angel, seed, Series X round, etc, you do set certain expectations for investors.[43] From our experience, you can easily lose investor interest just by using the wrong term to describe your round, even if that investor would have invested otherwise. Think about it – when you say 'Series A', investors, on the whole, immediately think '$1 million ARR'. Time is a precious commodity and if you do not show the expected metrics, more often than not, they will simply move on to the next opportunity, rather than spend energy trying to understand exactly *what* stage you are at. There are always exceptions, but it's best to stick to fundraising 'rules'.[44]

At the early stage, as aligned with the business-development cycle, your job is to show potential investors how you will (dis-)prove your hypothesis in the least expensive way, as fast as possible. Or in operational terms – focus on lowering your burn rate (a rate at which a company is losing money[45]) and increasing cycle iteration speed while always measuring the progress.

All investors look at the following fundamentals: people, market, product and traction. The difference is only in what order and to what extent. The later stage you are, the more you will need to demonstrate measurable proof and predictable progress (as opposed to vision or plans), in each of these categories to fundraise successfully.

The various structural types of investor and smart money tends to mainly come from:

- **Angels**. These are the people who have been founders themselves, are experts in their field and sometimes even VCs investing in a personal capacity. Angels invest their own personal money. Investments are usually aligned with government tax incentives.
- **Family funds**. Similar to angels, but usually with a bigger ticket size. They invest through a family wealth vehicle.
- **Institutional VCs**. Institutional investors usually have prior operational or founding experience themselves, or come from a very business-oriented background. VC funds are usually made up by limited partners, who themselves are either angels or family funds. Investments are usually aligned with a specific fund's lifetime.
- **Corporate VCs**. Corporates that have their own investment arm. Goals vary from strategic to purely financial investments. Funding usually comes from the parent company's balance sheet on a rolling basis (evergreen funds).
- **Rolling funds**. This is the latest type of US-based funding structure.[46] They are made up of accredited investors, including other founders, and are open ended (i.e. no 'fund size' target), and vary in ticket sizes. They are focused on investment process efficiency and speed to close.

There are many other ways to get your company funded, including bank or peer-to-peer loans, initial coin offering, research, commercial or governmental grants, invoice factoring, etc. Understand what is right for you at what stage and aim to have access to multiple funding sources at once – stuff that no one ever predicted *will* happen.

Understand what type of investor works best for you. Focus on what value they can bring beyond just money and be comfortable in holding them accountable to any promises. Examples are:
- Past experience in launching, scaling and exiting a company?
- A portfolio of companies with strong synergies or potential customers?
- Relevant industry players (customers, partners, influencers, etc) on a first-name basis?
- A network of relevant immediate hires?
- Their personal time?
- Other investors to the round?

There are also many ways to structure the funding itself (e.g. straight equity deal, loan arrangement against assets or royalty payback, etc). Whatever structure you go with NEVER EVER take any funding, no matter how small or how 'risk free' it might look, secured against your own personal assets. Liability *must* stay with the company so make sure that your company's legal structure can support that.

On the whole, if investors are interested in anything other than the equity, they are unlikely to be well aligned with your company's long-term goals (i.e. growth at scale). Some corporate investors will claim that they provide a 'strategic alignment' (whatever that actually means!) and sometimes even that they will 'teach you' about the industry, but be wary – you want investors who are interested in pursuing the same growth goals as you. If everyone's focus is aligned towards building great things, this will deliver more.

Craft the pitch

If you followed the business-development process, you should already have all the information you need for an investment meeting. Now, your job is to tell the story of why you are the next big thing. You need to demonstrate that there is a big problem and convince investors that you are the right people to solve it.

There is no 'standard' structure to pitch decks, nor any rules as to what specific medium or format they should be (e.g. a PDF document, wiki page or an investor memo), but focus on the four key areas mentioned earlier: people, market, product and traction. If you are a first-time founder, it's best to stick with the 'classic' approach to pitching – a PowerPoint deck. Note down all of your assumptions related to the market and the business and keep them handy during all conversations with investors. Be clear, yet detailed, and always factual; build a story and keep in-depth information in the appendix or footnotes/endnotes.

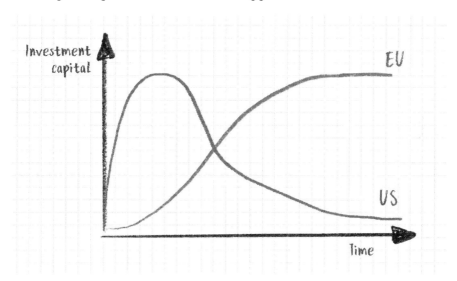

Difference in investment approaches between the US and EU investors. US investors tend to frontload most of the investment upfront and then only continue backing 'winners', whereas EU investors tend to wait until 'winners' emerge and then back them strongly.

Different investor regions tend to prioritise different areas. For example, US investors look primarily at the team, market potential and vision and most capital is therefore invested at the early stages, with a focus on rapid hypothesis testing and iteration, killing companies that do not show significant early traction. EU investors, on the other hand, tend to leave early companies to natural selection and rally behind companies with proven commercial traction. Neither approach is better or worse, they are just different strategies. It is expected to have several deck versions to match specific investor interest areas, adjusting your story and the ask accordingly.

So what should your pitch deck include?

People
1. What is your background, and more importantly, why you are the right team to execute this business?
2. What special insights or an unfair advantage do you/your team have?
3. What are your past business successes and failures (important to highlight lessons learned)?
4. What is your motivation for running this business? Will you persist when push comes to shove?
5. How well are you connected within the customer industry?
6. What is your plan for hiring, and who?
7. What advisors do you have? Only mention them if they have delivered truly exceptional value (and make sure to run it by them first!).

Market
1. What problem are you addressing?
2. For who it is a problem?
3. How do you know it is a real problem, rather than a solution looking for one, and how did you approach learning about it?

4. How big is the problem? How do you measure that?
5. Who else is solving the problem? How and where? What is their traction?
6. How big is the market opportunity? TAM and SOM? Note that market size is not the same as the problem size. For example, global warming is probably the biggest problem humankind is facing right now, but it is unlikely that you will get funded, other than by governmental research grants, to solve it.
7. What does an ideal customer look like?
8. What is your vision (prediction) for the market? What is the supporting evidence? How will you measure that?

Product

1. What is your solution to the problem? Review at a high level – not feature-by-feature.
2. How do you know – or will test – if it is the right solution? How do you measure that?
3. What intellectual property do you have?
4. Why is your product or approach better than the existing solutions? How do you measure that?
5. Can you show your product live with a customer, or at least a demo?
6. How are you positioning your product within the wider market? Why would customers use you, or even look at you, rather than your competitors?
7. How are you reaching your customers and generating leads?

Traction

1. What are you focused on for the near future? What's your MOM?
2. How will you make money? When? What does a two-year commercial projection look like?
3. What do your margins and unit economics look like? How will

that change over time? Be specific on your current pricing – explain how you got to it.

4. What is your traction to date? Detail anything that shows progress and validation – revenue (repeatable and not), pilots with conversion to production, user activity metrics, referrals, retention, etc. How did that grow month-on-month? Remember, no vanity metrics!

5. What does your sales pipeline look like? What funnel stages do you have?

6. What stage is each of your potential customers in the pipeline at? What needs to happen for each of them to progress or convert?

7. How much does it cost, on average, to acquire a single customer?

8. What customers have you lost? Why?

9. What are your medium-term customer acquisition plans?

Operational

1. What is your current burn rate by function (general and admin, R&D, operations, sales, marketing, legal)?

2. What cash do you have in the bank and other assets (stock, debtors, creditors) – i.e. the net balance sheet position?

The ask

1. What are you asking for? Keep it to a cash figure (without suggesting valuation or a shareholding amount). As a rule of thumb, each round is for the new investors to hold approximately 20% of your company on a fully diluted basis. Of course, that figure depends greatly on the competition that you can create between investors.

2. What is your funding progress so far? Who has committed and how much?

3. If you have a lead investor, what are the terms? How much of the round is still open?

4. What does an ideal investor look like? Who would you like to be introduced to? Be specific – check who the investor you're talking to is connected to on LinkedIn or appears often with (e.g. in joint podcasts, articles, reports, etc).

Do not hide metrics where you are not doing well. Investors are smart and they will uncover everything there is to know about your company, only for you to lose personal credibility. Include all the relevant metrics as part of the deck, without sugar coating. And make it very clear what you are doing *now* to improve any less-than-optimal metrics, and what your projections for them are.

Having two decks works best, in our experience – one to send before the meeting (but only once the meeting's been confirmed) and present on the day, and a second to share after the meeting, with much greater detail, including assumptions, approach and any other notes – which would then be circulated internally within the fund or group. Both decks need to stand on their own: the goal of the first one is to make people want to learn more, while the goal of the second is to convince anyone who has not even seen you or your pitch to invest. Both decks need to be based on factual metrics. Aim for 12 slides at most and keep your delivery to 10 to 15 minutes max. Go wild with the appendix.

Clarity is crucial – investors will assume that if you have trouble explaining the opportunity to them, you will likely struggle with customer interactions too. Quantify everything what you say and what you hear. Observe what clarifications investors ask for most and on what topics they spend most of the time, then keep reworking your deck based on the feedback. Remember, the pitch is not a one-way presentation, but a relationship building activity. Sometimes investors can have great insights, introduce you to advisors and customers or simply challenge you in ways that can improve your own processes, irrespective of whether they end up investing or not.

Maximise the fundraising process

Treat the fundraising process just like business development: segment your investors into priority groups and listen more than you talk. Aim to speak to 50 plus investors and have four to six actively interested leads.

Pitching and the resulting investment is a two-way street. Be confident in asking questions to measure cultural fit – you will be spending a lot of time with these people during board meetings. At AimBrain, we ended up selecting term sheets that had slightly worse financial terms, but a much better cultural fit with the team behind it, and this paid dividends over the years and we had help above and beyond our expectations.

It is almost a paradoxical statement to make, but investors are not interested in you, until they are. The default investor state is a 'no' – it is your job to create competition and make investors feel that not investing in you would be *their* loss. In operational terms, investors are making a bet that your company is undervalued *today* – you need to demonstrate that. That being said, do appreciate that investors have fiduciary duties to their partners or their own investors, so as soon as it is clear that you are unlikely to be the next big thing, their focus will shift to their portfolio front-runners. In operational terms, investors do not care about how *many* companies do 'well' in their portfolio (which is a vanity metric), they only care about the fund's overall dollar returns, which is why it makes sense that they want to dedicate most of the energy to their top three or four best performing companies. Front-runners can and do change over time – it is your job to make sure that your company is always one of them.

Each investor will have their own investment process, but it generally follows this workflow:

1. Initial meeting (relationship building and learning about each other).
2. Follow-up meeting(s) (pitch, demo, deep dives, pitch to partners).
3. Term sheet negotiation (subject to due diligence).
4. Due diligence (customer references, legal background checks, exclusivity period).
5. Closing (milestone and metric setting, legal signing, money transfer).

Assume it will take six months from your first investor meeting to full close – faster if you create competition between investors, slower if you have just not hit all the milestones.

Be comfortable with going into great detail about your business without an NDA in place. Investors see many founders and pitches every day and it would be unreasonable for them to sign any NDAs. Besides, their brand is much more valuable than any NDA, and if they step out of line, founders will take notice.

Some investors will have an 'investment thesis' related to either specific background founders, market or technology. Others will be more general, with a focus on traction, market size, growth and team. The investors social media and branding will often be explicit about where their focus is. Both are valid approaches so make sure you understand how well you fit into their existing portfolio. Look for information in the public domain (presentations, blog posts, tweets, etc) or their past investments. The magic happens when there are synergies between yourself and their existing investments (potential partnerships, the possibility to become customers of each other, etc).

The first term sheet is always the hardest.

Only term sheets count. Thinking that you 'only need a lead investor' to close the round is doing you a disservice. This is the same as hoping that customers will convert without any measurable indication that they will – do not spend energy other than keeping them updated with your progress at a high level. Until you have a term sheet on the table, any 'interest' is just a nice way of investors telling you that they are not convinced enough to set the terms themselves, but if you find someone who will do that, they would like to keep an option to review them, and maybe participate in the round. Remember, investments are just like sales – to win, turn individuals into your champions by understanding them within *their* context (see Chapter Eleven).

Closing a round with a single term sheet is good, but it does not leave you with a lot of leverage. Investors talk, so you cannot bluff your way through (most of the time). As a rule, having three or more term sheets puts you in a very strong position to negotiate your valuation. Do mind that raising too much too fast or at too high valuation without substance will set you up for failure as you will always be playing catch-up. Understand what is important for you and the company, as it is not always cash or its valuation.

Best foot forward

Do not confuse market with opportunity. It doesn't serve your best interests to present a simplistic view of the market, for example, by using a line from a report and stating that 'Dental hygiene is a $7 billion market and we only need 1% of that to make a huge business'. Investors will always dig deeper. How is that market broken down? Which of the specific areas do you address? What alternatives can the customer compare you to? If you are not prepared for these questions, the silence can fill the room. Sometimes the right answer is that 'we do not know yet'. Be clear, the size of the industry is not your *addressable* market (see Chapter Thirteen). Do not conflate the market, break it down into what you know and discuss those assumptions together.

Do not make sweeping generalisations. 'So who are you selling to?' 'Financial services.' 'Yes – but what part of financial services?' 'Well, all of it.' This exchange only tells the investors that you do not really know what your target market is. Investors want to know if you're targeting wealth management or the IT operations team in financial services. Is it the CIO or the operations leader? Is it the head of new product growth? Be specific as to what role within a specific category of industry. This will often be a starting point and will certainly grow into adjacencies in the future, but start at the most targeted customer. The same applies to any other statements you make – the more specific and measurable, the better.

Do not present a pipeline as the truth. One of Siobhan's roles before Episode 1 Ventures was two years in sales operations, covering a $1.5 billion portfolio of business across 23 countries with a 500+ person sales team. We're talking weekly, monthly, quarterly and annual sales commits, covering nearly every excuse for pipeline health, slowness in sales conversion between stages and deals shifting for various customer reasons. So when you present a pipeline and the investor asks deeper questions, know that they're simply trying to understand what is actually real. Pipelines evolve – they have sensitivities built in that are not always obvious. Innovation budgets and pilots are not always representative of what will move into production. Share the truth of the relationship to enable an open discussion between you and the investor if you can envisage working together.

Do not hold out for a hero. 'Hiring an experienced sales person' is not a plan to improve your sales. It is not a bad thing, but it is a timing thing. At seed stage, you should be focused on founder-led sales, getting to a deep understanding of your customer, their pain points and what value you bring. Once you see and understand patterns in the value you bring, and your proposition resonates frequently with customers, then it is the right time to bring in the first commercial hire. It is a common discussion during the VC pitch – what is the right talent plan in the seed to Series A journey. It differs depending on the type of startup, industry focus and maturity. Be open to that discussion – it will help you to align expectations from all sides.

Know 'why you'. Some investors like asking questions like 'What if Google/Facebook/BigCompany decides to do it too?'. It's a legitimate question. To answer it, understand what it actually means (hint: market validation), your strengths (hint: speed, customer support, flexibility, ability to target specific target markets) and track record or proof points (hint: paying customers, retention rates). Similarly, think about 'Why has this not been done before?' and 'What is your defensibility (or moat)?'. The former is all about helping potential investors to understand the market and your unfair advantage, while the latter is all about showing your thinking at scale (e.g. building and leveraging network effects).[47] You might not have proven answers today, but it is important to show a convincing path for how you will get there.

Fundraising gotchas

Reaching out to VCs. From our experience, you need to reach out to someone at mid-level seniority at the fund. Reach out to someone too low and your deck will be simply compared against a table of 'good metrics' without any consideration to vision; contact someone too high up and they will simply ignore your outreach because you were not pre-qualified. Aim for the mid-seniority level. This applies only to large funds, of course. Smaller teams (up to five) usually do everything themselves, from lead sourcing to investment decisions. The goal is to get a meeting, not a commitment.

Brokers. From our experience you want to deal with investors yourself and not go through a proxy or a broker. Investors appreciate that you want to get your hands dirty and given that they will be giving you their money and their time, they want to get to know you as an individual, from the very first interaction.

Projections. Everyone knows that projections are out of date as soon as you hit 'save' on that spreadsheet, but what is important is to show your thinking process. Often, people will have different ideas from their own experience and other fields that could be useful to you.

Fund lifetime. Understand exactly where the fund is in its lifecycle. Investors usually raise multiple funds with the expectation to return it over the ten-year horizon to their investors. Coming too late into a specific fund might mean that you get pushed to exit or raise another round sooner than you would otherwise like.

'No' can mean 'not yet'. Even if a particular investor does not participate in the round, they can still bring you a lot of value. Introductions to other investors, customers or industry experts are as valuable as cash. As the song goes: 'Ask for money, get advice. Ask for advice, get money twice'.[48] Expect most investors to pass on your opportunity – that does not reflect badly on you. However, always observe the patterns. If most investors are focusing on the same problem area, you might want to revisit your pitch, metrics or the hypothesis.

Legals. Take your time and fully understand what right of first refusal, veto rights, drag-along rights, information rights, board observer rights and clawback rights mean. You will want some (e.g. drag-along) and definitely not want some of the others (e.g. sole investor veto rights). There are significant implications depending on who you raise from and what your company's situation is. There are a lot of horror stories from founders who took money without fully understanding the conditions it came with. Equally, there are many stories of founders not including clauses that later would have been beneficial. For example, if a corporate investor asks for 'right of first refusal', it might make sense – after all, if you have an offer on the table and your existing shareholder can match it, what is the problem? Maybe it is even an advantage since you already know each other? Well, it turns out the clause has non-obvious secondary effects: acquirers usually do not progress if they see the clause, as it means they might spend energy valuing your company, for your corporate investor to just match the offer with no effort on their side. You just decreased the odds of your own success. Always consult with lawyers, ideally through recommendations from fellow founders.

Dilution. Investors want to see that you care massively – are *obsessed* – about your company. If your incentives are not aligned with the investor's, it is unlikely that you will weather all the storms. Aim to retain 70% to 80% of company shareholding between all founders before your Series A. Any less than that and investors will seriously question if you have enough skin in the game, and will sometimes pass on the opportunity. If your capitalisation table is less-than-ideal and your investors have a target percentage ownership, ask them to buy out earlier investors so they do not dilute the founders too much. If both sides agree, it is a win-win, with your angels making a guaranteed return early. As a last resort, have a conversation about buying back shares if the company meets some specific performance targets.

Costs. Agree a fixed all-in cost with lawyers for closing the round. Many lawyers will pitch a percentage of the pricing structure, but we are yet to hear of a lawyer who actually increased the company's valuation. There should not be any costs from the investors upfront – make sure you get that in writing when learning about their process, because we have heard about founders being invoiced for 'time' from not-so-reputable funds or individuals. On the other hand, do expect to pay for third-party due diligence (usually your specific industry experts hired independently to give their opinion) and lead investor legal expenses, but ONLY from the monies received from the investment. Ask your lead investor to cap their legal fees too, as part of the term sheet. Your lawyers will usually facilitate an escrow and fees will be distributed before you receive the final amount. If you have a competitive round, many costs can be negotiated out.

Secret sauce. If you are a deep-tech or otherwise IP-heavy company, under no circumstances disclose exactly how you do it – your secret sauce. Investors talk, remember? So assume that investors will share your deck with their peers. Some of those peers will have a direct interest in your competitors (e.g. through angel investment). Therefore you also need to assume that all of your competitors will see your deck too. Do not put your secret sauce in writing, not even during the due diligence stage.[49] You need to show proof that it works, and growth plans, without disclosing exactly *how* it works. Focus on metrics and share any other observable items (e.g. your focus regions, verticals, etc).

CHAPTER SIXTEEN
Find the right incentives

One of the many reasons why Venture Capital and investment capital is successful is the true alignment of incentives. The VC or investor invests in companies that will deliver a return to their investors, and the VC/investor manager makes a percentage of carry of that fund.[50] If the company grows well with the funding, everyone who has equity wins a piece. The same is true inside the business-development cycle with your team: create a culture and incentives that drive a 'we win' mindset. This aligns the short, addictive nature of human beings with the long-term reward of high performance. You will want to craft different incentives for your founding team than for your commercial team.

Founding team reward and incentives

Getting the founding team setup right is as important to the success of your company as talking to your customers. Starting a company with someone is a lot like (and often even more involved than) a marriage. You are likely to spend around the same amount or more of your waking time with your co-founder as you are with your life partner.

Unless you have already worked with someone on starting a company together, it is very hard to predict how people will behave in unstructured environments while under a lot of stress. Even if you have been long-term friends or work colleagues, startups is just another league. Unlike in marriage, you cannot 'date' your co-founder first to see how it goes. The founding team needs to commit fully to each other from day one and that is scary. You want to de-risk as much of your execution as possible – check talent investors who focus on facilitating the process.[51]

Trust. Founding teams are all about trust – you simply do not have time to manage or be managed by your co-founder. Shit will happen, and you and your co-founder will inevitably make mistakes along the way. The key is to appreciate that everyone is doing their best – there is no place for blame, only for reflection and improvement. Blaming your peers is a sure way to demotivate them. Also appreciate that sometimes people will have ups and downs – that is completely normal. There will be weeks where you contribute ten times as much as your co-founder and there will be weeks where they contribute ten times as much as you. However, what is not OK if any of the founders under deliver *constantly* and you find yourself taking on their responsibilities. In such cases, it is necessary to have an honest conversation about whether the company is still a good fit for them. Being upfront with your motivation and goals is also part of building trust. What drives you? What do you want to achieve? How big do you want to grow the company? What positions and responsibilities do you see yourself part of – now and in the future? How well is everyone aligned? Share and ask for any potential issues or reservations upfront. We have seen a few companies that failed simply because one of their founders decided that their previous nine-to-five job paid better and left the team. Startups are NOT a get-rich-quick scheme – all statistics are against you.[52] Create a contingency plan and know your risk boundaries for your ongoing financial commitments (e.g. a mortgage) and communicate that with the team to set expectations. Problems arise when founder goals are fundamentally incompatible with each other and trust is destroyed when said goals come as a surprise.

Equity. How to split equity between founders is probably one of the most frequently asked questions on the startup scene. There are many approaches and many ways to overcomplicate it. However, one thing is for sure – do not leave it 'for later' or 'when we raise our first round'. You absolutely need to have the hard conversation upfront. If not resolved early, at best it will become a distraction due to the uncertainty, and it is more than likely to create resentment if the later allocation does not meet original expectations.

At AimBrain, we split all founder equity equally – 50/50. It served us well and we never had to revisit the topic. While 50/50 is a *simple* solution, it is in no way unintentional. Sharing equity equally means that you can hold each other to the same high standards and responsibility. It removes all mental excuses for feeling like you should work more or less than your partner. As a consequence, there is no unhealthy competition: you do the best you can and you trust that your partner does so too. If you do not think that equity should be split equally, or that people have taken different amounts of risk, which needs to be reflected between the founders, consider whether they should be your co-founder or a strategic employee/early hire instead. Equal split means equal skin in the game. It means success is everyone's responsibility *uniformly*. After all, sometimes it is healthy to have your ass kicked by your founder as a reality check, but this can only be effective if all founders are equal. On the other side of the coin, be mindful of situations where it is the co-founder themself who suggests a lower split in exchange for a higher salary or a part-time role to leave space for consulting or side gigs for personal benefit – are they as committed as you think? Make sure founder shares have a vesting schedule. You do not want someone leaving the company with shares that could have been used with strategic hires. Four years with a one-year cliff is standard, and don't be surprised if during significant rounds you are asked to restart your vesting (although you can negotiate it out if you have multiple term sheets).

Compensation. Founder salaries vary significantly depending on your traction, fundraising, stage, etc. As a general rule, in the early days, pay yourselves enough that you are not distracted by money problems, but not enough to be able to afford luxury items from the salary alone. Your wealth is in the company's equity. You will liquidate that at an exit event or along the way (e.g. a secondary sale) if you do well. To grow the company early, you need to keep as much cash in it as you can; that is the 'rocket fuel'.

Titles. Truth is that, in the early days, all founders will contribute to many areas of the business. A CEO will need to know what's happening with the product and manage it, a CTO will need to be customer facing and handle customer support. Titles will not matter much, but they are important nonetheless. People, i.e. your customers, are used to structure and title connotations – your goal is to remove any confusion about who they should be contacting to discuss the commercial agreement and who to connect with their implementation team. Just as with equity conversations, agree on focus areas, and thus matching titles, early on. However, keep titles out of company decision making – 'We should do X because I am the CEO' is a sure way to build poor internal culture.

Commercial team reward and incentives

The commercial team is different to the founding team, who hires them. Sometimes the commercial team will be brought into an employee option scheme and share in the upside equity – at a different rate to the founders, of course, but still aligned to sharing in the bigger vision of the company. Therefore, you want to deliberately design rewards (equity, to be achieved after the work) and incentives (short term, to be achieved during the work). To craft the right rewards and incentives. Think of it as a series of experiments with people, incentives and strangely varying behaviours to get to your first ten enterprise customers. From AimBrain and other experience, two major factors have an influence here: create a **customer-led culture** that has **flexible goals**.

Create a customer-led culture

- Sales and early business-development people will challenge management or founder decisions. Be aware that this can very easily take you on the wrong path if you listen to them, rather than to the customer directly yourself. Put the customer voice first.

- Software engineers respect good sales people, especially where the proof is in customer numbers and not how confident or loud the person is. Prioritise the outcome, results, rather than 'effort'.
- Nail down the customer qualification stage. A big funnel is nice and makes everyone feel good, but if it does not convert it's a huge energy waster. The goal is getting to ten enterprise customers, not creating 1,000 contacts at a 1% conversion rate.
- Find business-development and sales people who care about PMF rather than purely the sales numbers; even if you had EXTREMELY good foundations, the wrong salesperson can take you off track. Assess their cultural fit and their focus on early sales.

Set flexible goals

- Sales are absolutely CRUCIAL for scaling the company! So reward for success. Pay lower in percentage (commission) until they meet their targets, and then scale.
- Before you hire a new salesperson, agree on quarterly goals for the full year and become driven by them. Give them three months and fire them immediately if they do not perform. The longer you keep them around, the more it will cost you monetarily, and overall in terms of the company's morale. To say that the product is not working, or that they need more time to learn, are just excuses. Ensure you have a six-month probation on all new hires, and do your check-in at three months. A good salesperson will add value on the day they sign their employment contract.
- Salespeople tend to not want to commit to specific metrics, only 'best effort' – your job is to measure them. Be mindful of a commission structure; it's very common for salespeople to be unhappy with a commission structure, whatever it is. They will

always try to play the metrics, rather than focus on what's best for the company. Therefore, have a team goal and individual incentives. Adjust the commission plan as your company goals change (e.g. a bonus payout on raising the next round of funding), and always focus on non-vanity metrics. Split commission between new customers and renewals. Be very specific about what your goals are – salespeople will get you leads that are not relevant, but fit the criteria, and will moan about their motivation if you do not reward them.

In setting the customer-led culture and flexible goals, watch out for the following behaviour and think carefully about how to deal with it:

- Be wary of bringing in commercial people too early – salespeople can only work if you give them the right tools and an understanding of your business-development cycle, as outlined in ACT I.

- Commercial people are very motivated by their commission and there will be a constant battle between commercial people and the product team. Commercial people will complain about selling things that do not exist or blame their lack of performance on product capabilities. All you can do is focus on the customer voice and manage the conversation. Be direct with your decisions.

- Keep an eye out for any commercial or salesperson who does not keep their notes in Salesforce up to date. They might use the excuse that it slows them down. Or they might use pressure tactics, like 'Do you want me to keep Salesforce updated or bring you new customers?.' They will end up doing neither. Scale is achieved by observing patterns. If you don't keep notes, it means there are no observations to analyse, which means you cannot establish a scalable process. Tracking is mandatory: the sales team must bring new customers, while documenting the progress.

- Watch out for salespeople who like to offload work to different people or teams (marketing, product or the founders). If you start questioning your salespeople, it's time to fire them. There is a difference between a salesperson and a business-development person. In the early days, you need someone who has a hybrid of these skills.[53] Salespeople are great at repeating a process, but poor at establishing what that process should be. A great business-development person will take the business-development cycle and create momentum; they'll craft the funnel, convert it, but will not be challenged (and thus motivated) if asked to constantly repeat the same sales process. So think about what needs your company has, and hire accordingly.

- When hiring, look for people with a track record of selling stuff without references or clients to rely on. Look for people who were the first and early hires at other successful companies. Prior experience of selling at an established company is irrelevant – instead look for people who can identify innovators and sell to them.

It might seem harsh at first, but we've seen these patterns again and again, from first-time founder hires to global sales teams. We are not saying that *all* salespeople will display such behaviour – we are simply giving you a heads up.

First commercial hires

When hiring your first commercial people, focus on what's important to get to their first ten enterprise sales:

- Know the top three things you need from the person. Is it the same top three things they need to have skills/network/experience in?

- Do they have a network that they can hire from?[54] If not, pass.

Top performers know that hiring is the hardest part and will always have a few people that they keep warm.

- Do they have a proven track record of Deers, rather than Elephants or Rabbits? It requires a certain type of personality to be able to deal with all the groundwork for Deers while resisting big cheques (and thus potentially big commission) from the Elephants.

- Can you see evidence of them as a closer with customer success, and as an upsell specialist, with deep product knowledge?

- You want the hire to have experience of working at the same stage as where your company is currently operating, as well as with the same target customer size (and ideally market).

The mechanics of flexible compensation structure

For a solid starting point, use the following mechanics:[55]

- Define eligibility: what is their degree of responsibility within the sales process? Define the specific types of customers they should target, but also give some flexibility to the commercial leads. Always ensure they are targeting within your key category, though. Don't have them signing partnerships that will generate no revenue for years – remember, energy is a finite resource.

- Keep a balanced mix of base and variable pay. For the first ten customers, use a system of performance levels: have a minimum threshold to hit (80% of plan), a target (100%) and then a higher target (150%). If anything is under 80%, pay 50% of the commission. If the team delivers above 80% but below 100%, then payout at 65%. This is to encourage focusing on achieving the 100% set target. If the team delivers 100%, then pay out on 100%. If the stretch plan is achieved – somewhere between 110% and 130% – then payout up to 150%.[56]

- Define no more than three performance weights and measures.

For example, customer name or key accounts you want to land, combined overall revenue target or number of contracts signed.

- Adopt a quarterly payout frequency – try to pay out as close to achieving the targets as possible to keep reward connected to achieving the goal.

- Ensure you have governance in place: outline that you/founders decide on the thresholds and payouts for each period in advance. Business development and sales will inform the beginnings of your sales-incentive plans. Involve the commercial team and be transparent in your decisions.

- Pay only from cash-received. As a young startup, cash is your lifeblood and you cannot afford to pay on contract signing, when (and if!) the money has not even reached you. We have seen customers pulling out of contracts in very creative ways – clawing back any commission in such an event from the salesperson would be very demotivating for everyone. Remember, negativity spreads like a wildfire (and people are generally pretty sensitive around the topic of money).

CHAPTER SEVENTEEN
Prepare for the future scale

With business fundamentals in place, you need to prepare for the future scale. While sales solve most problems, there is much more to a good and productive company. Below are some insights and processes that took us seven years to iterate.

Scale, just like product-market fit, is a process rather than an event. To get there, you'll need to focus on individual bottlenecks, rather than on overhauling whole processes. (The former is optimisation, the latter is procrastination.) You can go surprisingly far with a couple of broken processes, so never lose focus on what ultimately matters the most – providing and capturing value with customers.

Create a collective company culture

If you want to go fast, go alone. If you want to go far, go with a team. You need to build a crew that will enable the company to succeed – it is everyone's responsibility. You need to bring people in who are metrics-driven and ingrained with the build › measure › learn cycle mentality, whatever specific area or department they are in. The metrics-driven approach helps to focus everyone on improving what really matters. Sometimes it might feel like building metrics takes longer than actually doing work, so find ways to simplify the process while still showing momentum, and reward the desired behaviour or top performers. For example, instead of implementing advanced metrics for a full funnel tracking showing you hundreds of graphs that, let's be honest, you will never look at, focus on a few KPIs that matter. Hell, if you have no idea how to implement automated reporting in Salesforce, don't – simply keep updating the key numbers on a whiteboard and use the time you would have spent otherwise talking to customers. You will later either afford to have someone else automate the reporting or there will be no need for any reports.

Your company's culture and therefore its core values will change over time – that is a good thing. Only companies that adapt survive. Make sure to keep a very close eye on it though; as soon as you have internal politics or other toxic behaviour it will spread and amplify – people like to bring in more of the same type of people. The best teams we have seen are relentlessly customer-focused – they go above and beyond their job description or the support ticket at hand to make sure the customer is satisfied.

Internal culture will develop on its own, or it can be directed – but it should never be imposed by you. Review your values periodically with everyone and guide them based on the input. The best way for people to buy into the values is for them to create them to begin with. Make sure that you constantly communicate what the company stands for and why. Share real examples of uncertain situations where your values guided you towards the best outcome.

Your company is a team, not a family. Sometimes companies outgrow individuals and sometimes individuals outgrow companies. In either case, the best option for all sides is to part ways on good terms – misery propagates easily and you cannot afford to let it spread.

Assume that people will leave no matter how great your company is – and there is nothing you can do about it. Their circumstances change, things happen, preferences evolve. The best you can do is make sure that it does not come as a surprise, and that it leads to as little disruption as possible. You do not want engineers leaving in the middle of major deployment or commercial people in the middle of a major contract negotiation. Cultivate an open culture where feedback is encouraged, seen as an opportunity to improve and taken with the same appreciation, no matter the seniority – it is very detrimental to overall morale and demotivating for the individual if they feel that their feedback will be simply ignored by the 'management' or, worse, cause conflict.[57] We are not suggesting to jump for '360 reviews' or similar approaches – a simple direct conversation is where you start. However, make sure that people are open to feedback before you give it – make the recipient feel valued.[58]

The best metrics are based on milestones rather than timelines, so design your employment structure to support that. As a first thing with each employee, outline their role as a finite job based on completing mutually beneficial work units over a one- or two-year time period.[59] At the end of the work unit(s), reassess new priorities and alignment. This way, everyone knows what they are expected to deliver and is on the same page as to what they are looking for.

Always get people to have skin in the game. Is there a feature your engineers do not think they should be working on? Bring them in on a call and let them hear for themselves how it is impacting the customers. People need to see stuff firsthand. Do you need people to put in more energy than usual for an urgent, unexpected deadline? Buy them dinner in the office without setting any conditions or goals – trust your team to do their best. Always make sure you show appreciation.[60] But be mindful about asking them to work harder than usual so often that it becomes an expectation – people do burn out and needing to re-hire anyone unexpectedly is costly. After all, you want to build a culture where everyone recognises company priorities, appreciates the urgency and self-mobilises accordingly; it is impossible for you to always be there, constantly pointing out what is 'urgent and important'. Similarly, if *everything* is urgent and important you will quickly desensitise everyone and when the real shit hits the fan, there won't be anyone to help you clean it up.[61]

Focus only on a few key metrics that are relevant at that specific stage. Reiterate and make them visible to everyone. All initiatives and processes should relate back to them. At all times, all employees should know what metric they are focused on and why, and they should *understand* how their work is contributing towards improving it. Measure momentum and reward it.

Prioritise ownership and accountability. Great people will continue working outside the office and the core hours. Enable your team to have personal agency – you are paying them to achieve certain goals rather than to sit at a desk for a set number of hours. Measure progress and as long as everything is getting done you should not worry about how or when. Inversely, the best way to get rid of great people is to start micro-managing them. Your job is to provide the right tools, steer the direction and get out of the way. Any culture can *attract* great people, but only the right culture can *retain* them. Accountability goes both ways – make sure to hold regular all-hands town halls or Q&A sessions to answer any of their questions. Treat these as 'pulse checks' in terms of what is important to everyone and as a 'reality check' you.

Celebrate small wins. Startups are hard as it is and most people are giving much more behind the scenes than you can see. Life is not about big events – it is about all the daily, boring, routine stuff that is in between. Make sure to recognise teams and individuals for doing great work on a consistent basis and all the small improvements they've made on the way. Great people are motivated by their work providing real value. They can find a job anywhere – you need to make sure that they know they made the right choice, are making an impact and are appreciated. (In the same vein, never criticise anyone publicly – provide *constructive* feedback *privately* instead.) The day simply does not contain enough hours for you to know everything positive that goes on in your company, so build mechanisms that enable praise. For example make it a norm to 'call out' people positively on public internal chat channels; send monthly company-wide email where each team lists their individual contributors or overall achievements; or have demo days where a team or individual presents what they are working on, including their own personal side projects – but do not make this into a competition if you are seeing the same names every time, something is wrong – either the unnamed people are not contributing or their contributions are not being recognised, inevitably creating politics.

Be transparent in the company's position, but do not air its dirty laundry amongst the whole team. For example, customer deals falling through is part of doing any business, but not everyone will be comfortable hearing about it. For some, it will be worrying and demotivating. It is a balancing act – share too much information and people will spend too much energy worrying about things that are not significant. Share too little and they will lose trust or not appreciate the effort and energy that is required to make things happen. Set expectations ahead of time. For example, if you are fundraising explain that multiple investors taking a closer look at the company to evaluate it is part of any fundraising, process, but it does not mean that they will invest. Also share that you are looking at multiple potential avenues apart from just VC funding. Setting such expectations will remove any concerns that 'the ship is sinking' if they see investors who never return (when for you it was a completely expected part of fundraising all along). It also leaves other funding options open for you without coming across as if 'the fundraising has failed'. It is your job to make sure that everyone is focused on the metrics that matter in their own areas and that cannot happen if they are worried about the livelihood of the company, and are too busy thinking about all the negative things that *could* happen to them.

The most humbling lesson we learned about leadership is to listen to and believe in your team. You hired them because they are better than you at what they do. So set a clear direction and get out of their way.

Build the founder mindset

Founding a company is hard and it doesn't get easier – problems do not change, only their scale does. While it might not be immediately obvious, people around you do pick up on your mood, your actions and your reactions – all without even saying a single word.[62] This then gets propagated and amplified throughout the company[63] and, if repeated multiple times, will become part of your culture. Be mindful of throwaway comments or even simple suggestions – people can take them much more seriously than you expect.

Your company is not your baby. Your company is not you either. Things will go wrong because of your decisions and you will be put under pressure with questions you have no answers to. Being calm and measured in your responses becomes increasingly important over time. You will be completely lost on what to do next, likely multiple times in the same day. Remember, try to be less wrong rather than right. Work with your team to make the best decisions you can fast and recover quickly if they turn out to be wrong. The less disruption to your business flywheel the better. Your decisions need to reflect what is best for the company, rather than for you or your board.

Accept that sometimes you can outgrow the company and sometimes the company can outgrow you. The leadership skills that are needed change all the time. Understand where you add the most value and, while extremely hard, learn to let go of your ego. Fundamentally, the better the company does, the better off everyone, including you, will be. If a title matters more to you than measurable success, reconsider if you are the right person to found a company in the first place.

Take care of yourself. Mentally and physically. You can build a great company without sacrificing your health, but you cannot lead a company while ill. Surround yourself with supportive peers, including other founders – this is so important for helping you keep your sanity. Celebrate everyone's wins and problem-solve everyone's issues. As it is said, startup is a marathon, not a sprint – so make sure you do not burn out before the finish line. Blocking out time for yourself is mandatory.

It is a wild ride with extreme highs and extreme lows. A positive, *measured* attitude will go a very long way. Always try to reframe negative thoughts or situations to your advantage. Something failed? Well, you just learned that something does not work – now you can be more efficient in the future. Lost a client? It's a learning opportunity to improve the experience you provide for existing customers, and when onboarding new customers. A founder has left? Better now than later – the longer people stay when they shouldn't, the bigger the damage they leave behind. Full inbox of emails you need to respond to? Great – no one talks to a dead company. Some days will just suck – and that is OK. Focus on the next action items in your control and keep that business flywheel moving.

The best productivity secret is: just get started. Physically, get in a work position and do the absolute minimum unit of work – you have just done the hardest part and started the productivity flywheel! Remember, objects in motion tend to stay in motion.

As a founder, you will also need to get good at context switching – within a single hour you will go from talking to a customer, to dealing with a legal issue and then to listening to employees who want more plants in the office – all important topics.

Finally, ignore the media noise – focus only on measuring and improving your own success.

Always be recruiting (and sometimes hiring)

Hiring is probably the biggest universal problem startups face. Why? Because you want to hire great people. However, there are only so many great people on this planet and great people are almost never looking for a job – and are rarely motivated by money alone. As such, you need to be constantly looking out for them and learning what makes them tick.

You should aim to spend 50% of your time recruiting, hiring and retaining great people. The difference between recruiting and hiring is that the former is all about building long-lasting relationships with great people and making them part of your network so when you need their specific expertise, you know immediately who to reach out to. Hiring, on the other hand, is all about making sure that they are the right people – for a specific position, and for your company's current situation – through a defined process.

You will make hiring mistakes. Repeatedly. Make sure that you have a legal probation period built-in as part of your employment agreements. As cold as it might seem (because no one goes into a relationship expecting it to fail), it is your job to make sure that if it does fail, the damage is minimal. As they say, hire slow, fire fast. Never hire or start a company with people you want to remain friends with. It worked out between myself and Alesis, but that is an exception to the usual outcomes we've seen from other founders. From our experience, your team will know before you if it was a bad hire, but it will be up to you to figure it out in a timely manner. Great people get very demotivated if forced to work with mediocre talent. You will be judged as a founder on how good you are at hiring great people, as much as how you are at firing them. We have seen people get angry, cry or threaten legal action – it sucks. Build a standardised hiring process and use it for all candidates – no matter how recommended they come. Charisma is a real thing, which hopefully you will learn to identify for what it is – having a standardised process will help you to avoid your own bias.

There is a huge difference between good and great people. Good people will be able to take what you have and repeat it or improve it to a good standard. Great people will create ideas that blow your mind – show things and create connections that are not obvious, that you have not even considered. Their direct contribution to the success of the company is ten times that of good people. They finish what you asked them to do and ask for more well ahead of the deadline. They measure themselves and discuss with you what they learned and how they will improve. They are more *constructively* critical of themselves than you are. Of course, all of that comes at a cost and you must learn to retain them effectively (but that is a book of its own!).[64] This is why hiring slow (finding great people *at the right time*) and firing fast (recovering from your mistakes quickly) is crucial – it has a compounding effect. Spend as much time learning about the candidates' capabilities as you do checking for cultural fit – it is a two-sided process.

Protect intellectual property

Just as with commercial contracts, do the same for employment agreements, internship positions or contractors: make it absolutely certain that the company owns all of the IP from the very first hire or interaction. For employees, reiterate how it works as part of your onboarding process too.

If you are ever targeted by a patent troll, the first thing to do is seek legal advice from someone who has experience of dealing with that type of dispute. Do not respond to the patent troll or acknowledge their communication until you have spoken to your lawyers. It is sensible to limit what goes in written communications (including emails) with your lawyers or anyone else to avoid the possibility that someone might try to misinterpret something you have said and compromise your legal position. While you are small it does not matter much, but as soon as you get bigger or start announcing customer wins or big funding rounds, everyone will want part of your success – and patent litigation is a very expensive matter in terms of both cash and your energy.

Make sure that your tech stack and any software you use (including product fonts!) has commercially friendly licences attached. Track them over time and review each new tool, item or library before using it. Later stage investors or potential acquirers will ask for this. You do not want to find out during acquisition discussions that the GitHub repository that you used very early on to generate a single testing dataset was not licensed for your commercial use.

Be customer-centric

As soon as you have a product, you will need to support its potential and existing customers. Superior customer service is a real differentiator – make sure that you use it to your advantage. Each customer request is an opportunity to wow your potential customers and remind your existing ones how good you are and that they made the right decision.

Initially, it will be you and your top people answering all the queries – make sure your team appreciates the importance of good and timely responses. Exposing non-customer-facing teams will help to drive customer-focused priorities – review all requests periodically and notice any patterns. Do not overcomplicate the whole process – it can be as simple as email.

Early on, measure satisfaction (e.g. on a scale of 1 to 5) and over time narrow down on what 'satisfaction' really means to your target market (e.g. time to first response, time to full resolution, support seniority, communication channel, communication style, etc). This will also set the framework, with real examples as the training material, and performance expectations for your future customer service team.

Make sure that the customer-service function is also measured and responsible for improving key company goals. Finally, appreciate the difference between customer service and customer support – the latter is about transactional interactions for fixing issues, the former is about building long-lasting relationships and cultivating happy customers around your brand.

Build sales partnerships

Focus on understanding the bigger picture of the customer ecosystem and therefore how partners play within it. Partners often play a bigger role at Series A and beyond – the scaling phase. For Seed companies, limit to what makes sense in a 12 to 18-month timeframe and work with a select one to establish trust and collective customer insight. Partners cannot sell for you – do not hold out for a hero.

- What type of partners does your industry have? What does a 'standard' arrangement (e.g. cost structure, margins, territories, etc) look like for each type? What are industry-standard partner metrics and costs?
- Why use Partner Strategy? What is the value exchange? How do you measure it?
- Top Partner Focus – which one brings the greatest value exchange for 12 to 18 months?
- What non-obvious incentives can you create or find? For example, a Cloud provider is incentivised for your account usage to grow, therefore you could leverage their sales team expertise and network (e.g. your target customers who are also their clients) when entering new regions.

Remember, if focus is on 'strategic' partnership, it usually means that you will lose money – even in the early days, treat the partner strategy with the same rigour as you do your go-to-market strategy.

Refine sales process

Keep your sales process simple for as long as you can. Focus on founder-led sales assisted by one to two Commercial Leads / Business Development Managers between your Seed and Series A stages. Limit your sales funnel to five stages, co-develop with customers and maximise energy towards achieving product-market fit.

Sometimes you will get bluebird (i.e. unexpected) deals coming in. There is always something that has been done by someone at some point to make it happen – it is never random. Find those actions and replicate – that email, relationship, newsletter – ask customers directly, understand and recreate.

Constantly evolve Success Metrics

Focus on what you need to achieve to prove product-market fit, showing progress on conversion rates over a 12 to 18-month time frame within the funnel and the evolution in customer types.

- Measure your funnel step conversion rates, adoption and engagement.
- Always know your total customer numbers, and how they are trending.

A successful go-to-market execution and product-market fit is more than just a revenue number. While the rule of thumb is to achieve £1million ARR for Series A, it is short sighted to rely only on that. The majority of investors at Series A will be looking for progress on the business model, your understanding of the market and proof of feasibility for future plans – i.e. having achieved £1 million ARR, can you *scale* it?

Cultivate the right mindset

Know and accept that you will have your plan and the reality will of course be more of an uphill battle than you expect. We have all felt this, figured out a way through and out of the dips. You'll want to fall in love with this process. It's an emotive one and, let's face it then figuring out how exactly you bring value to a customer in exchange for bankable revenue is why you exist. You are part of an infinite game to solve a problem, to bring a real solution that delivers outstanding value, that shifts and changes industries.

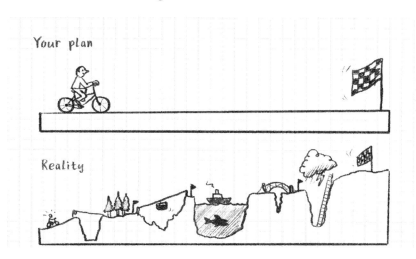

Reality is always a bigger uphill battle than you expect. Behind each 'overnight success' there are years of execution and uncertainty.

You will get it wrong many times, and every time that you do, it is an opportunity to learn.

- What did the customer actually say was valuable?
- What did the customer really mean?
- Why did the customer choose the alternative compared to our product/service offering?
- Does that mean we need to position/adapt for the next customer?
- How are we communicating vs what the customer is hearing?
- At the beginning, it is all about customer discovery. That translates into an understanding mindset. Work to understand where the real value actually is and priority level of a problem with your customer persona and market focus. Build that as a core of your company culture.

Scale without losing the personal touch

From customer discovery, you will move into an attempt to scale. This is effectively the cycle of product-market fit. During customer discovery, you've had personal interactions with the people you are delivering value to. They came to rely on your personal insights and you have walked the fine ledge between becoming a consulting business with technology and scaling for the technology business. Expect to answer:

- How do you provide the personal experience to customers supported by technology?
- What culture and values you are building into your whole team and their connections?
- Directly with the customer, collect feedback and review the changes in approach.
- What was the special 'magic' that keeps the customers returning?
- What product evolution do you need to have to address the customer experience? What does the roadmap look like?

Manage customer demands

At the beginning, you're focused on founder-led sales and often with technical founders, this means you have built an initial culture that is embedded in building the product out. Technical talent represents the biggest proportion of your overall budget and the team is building on customer input, without the demands of customer revenue. As you grow your commercial strength and revenues, expect that your customers are going to become more demanding, your new Product Manager/Commercial team will start to demand features and a product roadmap that will come into perceived and real conflict with the technical product build out.

Expect that you will need to:

- Evolve the product in line with company vision, whilst addressing customer demands.

- Learn how to say no to certain customer requests and manage expectations.
- Create an internal communication structure and culture for dealing with competing demands and being clear on decisions.

Overcome the hard part of enterprise sales

When you try your first GTM strategy, and it takes a year to play out on big enterprise clients because they will make decisions on a different timeline to you (slowly!), they seem to be making the right noises but those noises do not turn into recurring revenue. You realise you need to change something because you did not understand the customer pain quite as well as you thought. When building a deep-tech company and selling to enterprise clients, the feedback loop is much slower than some website that you can throw up and see if the clicks follow. Expect this simple fact – enterprise sales is really hard and there are many different reasons why it might be not working. The subject requires deeper attention and is outside of the scope for this book.[65]

Manage conflict

Startups are incredibly stressful environments – you will see the best and the worst that the people around you have to offer. And we do not mean only your co-founder or employee. We mean everyone – your family, your partner and your friends. We have seen spouses break up, founders leave and friends give up on the relationship. Just like learning to switch context quickly, it is essential that you learn to separate yourself from the company and work from your leisure time. It is your duty to everyone to take care of your health, otherwise it is a sure way to burnout.

You will have conflict, it is inevitable. Pay attention to your interactions and be sensitive to the four horsemen of the apocalypse (criticism, defensiveness, contempt and finally, stonewalling)[66] – while the original study was concerned with distilling the key behaviours that lead to divorce (to 93% accuracy!), from our experience, the principle applies equally well to relationships in general. The key here is not to avoid the confrontation, but to approach it constructively. If you avoid conflict, you starve yourself of a different point of view, one that is potentially better than yours. Similarly, if you are mean, people will choose to evade you – fights are not worth the energy.[67] More diverse teams make overall better business decisions,[68] but you have to want the feedback in the first place. Leave your ego out of it and focus on what is best for the company. If you mostly optimise for yourself, you simply cannot build anything that is bigger than you.

At AimBrain, we had a simple priority hierarchy that we would always follow when making decisions – it served us well over the seven years of running the company. Firstly, establish a common ground – define decision-making axioms:

1. It is never about an individual, it is about the company.
2. 'It has been done this way before' is a great way to never find a better solution.
3. 'I have done / used X in the past and it worked' – great, but it is very unlikely that we are in the exact same situation again.

Then follow a simple decision-making rule: logic arguments relevant to the specific situation trump emotions, preferences or wishes. However, not everything is logical in real-life situations – sometimes you just do not have the past experience or data to back up your position or instincts. If, after a discussion, there is still no consensus, follow whomever is the most invested in the situation. If all else fails, rock, paper, scissors – agree to any path as an experiment, then learn and iterate. The goal is to be decisive and progress (see Act III). I have heard a great expression by a fellow founder – 'disagree and commit'. Basically, there is no place for *compromises* in a startup – you either commit fully or not at all. Everything in between is a waste of energy as you will not be able to fully verify your hypothesis without a full commitment and alignment from everyone. As Ronald Reagan, American politician and 40th president of the USA, said, 'Peace is not absence of conflict, it is the ability to handle conflict by peaceful means.'

Keep the business flywheel momentum

People react to change rather than absolute values. It is important to keep accelerating more than just keeping the same pace. The worst position for a startup is to be a 'zombie' – not exactly failing, but not succeeding either. It is a place that makes you wonder every day if you should just stop and cut your losses or continue because you can just about taste the success, which is defocusing and hence unproductive. For employees, it is just a job – if they do not see growth, they will become anxious and unfulfilled. You will find it harder to retain existing and recruit new members. You will find that investors are no longer emailing you to check in on your progress. Buyers are no longer knocking on your door to talk about joint vision. You will feel reputational anxiety. Game over.

At any moment you are practising *something*. You could be practising playing games, relaxing, winning an argument, improving your physique, numbing your brain with TV or growing your business. Your most important job, the biggest responsibility that you carry for everyone, is to start the business flywheel and then continuously increase its momentum – make sure that you are practicing the right things.

ACT III

HOLDING OUT FOR A HERO

Throughout this entire book, we've focused on the tools, frameworks and methodologies for approaching research, as well as reaching out and engaging with customers. In some ways, that's the easy bit. At AimBrain, the biggest lesson we learned is that succeeding is a unique equation that is as much about the people, about understanding yourself and your own biases and about your ability to engage with other people to get to those ten enterprise customers.

In this final chapter, we focus on the 'who'. Everything we've outlined requires a person to do it. That person can come from any background, with any kind of experience, and approach the task of delivering the first ten enterprise customers in many different ways. You could be the founder of the business, the founder of the business unit or product group, or you could be the external person brought in to fix a broken company. In all of those roles, know that you will suffer and will need to get over the hero issue.

You may have noticed that throughout the book we used 'you/your/ yourself' much more than 'us/ours/ourselves'. This was not by accident – we did our best to share what we have learned first hand and all the mistakes we made, but it is up to you to make it work. YOU are the hero.

So, hero, before you embark or continue on your mission to take over the world, here are our parting pieces of advice.

Be aware of baggage

Whether you're the founder or a person coming in from outside the company, you know you have baggage. You might say 'I felt as if I'd been there, seen it, done it and felt the industry pain'. And with all your industry experience, market knowledge and laser insight, you might as well *be* the customer. Except you're not. You're coming at the problem with a whole bunch of assumptions that might be right – but are equally likely to be wrong. It's called assumptive bias and it can blind you to the *actual* needs of the *actual* customer. By believing what you see through the filter of your past experiences, your view doesn't necessarily match the reality of your customer base. The problem you are solving might not be one they actually have. The value you have put on a particular pain point might, in reality, be dwarfed by something far more pressing. The key failing here is not stopping to challenge your own preconceptions. You need to test your hunches and instinctive biases against the types and personas of the customers you are targeting. By identifying what their biggest challenges and pain points truly are, you can shape your product accordingly and train your focus on the highest-value customers.

Spotlight, but no illumination

There are many challenging parts to the business development process and it's hard getting them all working like a well-oiled machine. Pricing, transactions, demand marketing – if you can see an aspect that is problematic, it seems sensible to focus your energies on fixing and optimising it. The easy mistake to make here is to over-focus on that one spot and fail to see it as part of the wider, integrated whole. All the components in the sales process are related, with each having a bearing on the others.

Focus instead on the particular pain point you are trying to solve for your customer. You need to evolve your product to address that problem and doing so informs your sales process, not the other way round. I see companies placing too much emphasis on process or a particular part of it, citing tools such as Excel, SFDC and Pipedrive as their saviour. The specific tool is not the answer, a holistic approach is.

Don't hold out for a hero

When it's clearly so easy to get the emphasis and focus of your sales efforts wrong, it makes sense to bring in a guru who wouldn't make such mistakes. Someone who's been a CEO or a head of sales at firms they've built up and successfully sold. Hiring a sales expert with a glittering track record seems like a no-brainer, right? It means you and your co-founders can get back to the important work of developing your product, confident in the knowledge that sales will soon be going stratospheric.

Except your new sales hotshot doesn't have that same early-stage fire you have – the passion that has already engaged your first customers or development partners. They want to implement whatever drove those explosive sales for them, but they are probably still a little way off for your company. They'll call up their network and try and sell what they think your product should be, and will very likely lean on your engineers to bend it into that more familiar shape.

Failure is going to leave a bad taste for you and your dejected sales guru, with time and money down the drain. The truth is, founders remain the best salespeople for their products at the very early stage of a business. While a product is being shaped and crafted by working closely with customers.

Can't let it go

A mistake that's just as easy to make as handing off sales when your company is not quite ready, is not handing off sales soon enough.

Confusing? Well, striking this balance is tricky but important at such a crucial moment in the development of your business. Founder-led sales, aka business development, is enormously important and the best way of setting out with your customer at the heart of your organisation. There will come a point, though, when the time is right for hiring someone else, allowing the founders to focus on execution.

Straightening it all out

Perhaps the final potential mistake to avoid is to take these as singular pitfalls to look out for and address. In actual fact, these common problems are very often interlinked and can have a cascading impact that ends up in a tangled mess that's hard to unravel (see ACT I). The result can be a lack of traction that you can't understand because there is no one thing that is obviously wrong.

The stage your business is at, the level of customer development you have reached and the resources you have will all be factors affecting how you navigate past these common mistakes. The best approach is to focus on the customer group with the most significant pain point and make them the focus of your efforts.

You are the only one left

As the person driving this entity, you're the one who owns the task of solving it. This is on you: You bridge the gap in missing conversations. You drive it home! Getting to your first ten enterprise customers will demand all your drive, all your energy, your passion and instincts. We've shared our experiences, the tools, frameworks and methodologies to get there. Now YOU are the one who has to make it happen.

There is no set path to success, but there are tried and tested approaches that will help you to find it significantly faster. Hopefully our framework helps you to frame your mind and focus on the right things. Concentrate on building value rather than creating hype. The latter will come naturally as a result. You are in control of your own story, so:

Endnotes

[1] https://TheFounderHandbook.org/unicorn-startups

[2] https://TheFounderHandbook.org/death-of-a-salesman

[3] https://TheFounderHandbook.org/software-is-eating-the-world

[4] https://TheFounderHandbook.org/clarke-three-laws

[5] https://TheFounderHandbook.org/why-startups-fail

[6] https://TheFounderHandbook.org/crossing-the-chasm

[7] https://TheFounderHandbook.org/do-things-that-do-not-scale

[8] https://TheFounderHandbook.org/startups-are-a-marathon-and-not-a-sprint

[9] https://TheFounderHandbook.org/ode-to-the-founder

[10] https://TheFounderHandbook.org/when-to-stop

[11] https://TheFounderHandbook.org/startup-lean-canvas

[12] https://TheFounderHandbook.org/rubber-duck-a-business-processes

[13] https://TheFounderHandbook.org/problem-analysis-with-five-whys

[14] https://TheFounderHandbook.org/content-marketing

[15] https://TheFounderHandbook.org/why-brand-familiarity-matters

[16] https://TheFounderHandbook.org/vanity-vs-actionable-metrics

[17] https://TheFounderHandbook.org/listen-to-understand-and-not-just-to-respond

[18] https://TheFounderHandbook.org/respect-others-time

[19] https://TheFounderHandbook.org/the-mom-test

[20] https://TheFounderHandbook.org/rabbits-deers-and-elephants

[21] https://TheFounderHandbook.org/biggest-startup-failures

[22] https://TheFounderHandbook.org/doing-things-that-do-not-scale

[23] https://TheFounderHandbook.org/sunk-cost-and-fallacy-effect

[24] https://TheFounderHandbook.org/nothing-worth-doing-is-easy

[25] https://TheFounderHandbook.org/survival-of-the-fittest

[26] https://TheFounderHandbook.org/aligning-everyone-towards-a-common-goal

[27] https://TheFounderHandbook.org/zombie-startups

[28] https://TheFounderHandbook.org/startup-exponential-growth

[29] https://TheFounderHandbook.org/perceived-product-value

[30] https://TheFounderHandbook.org/intellectual-property-in-startups

[31] ROI ratio = (gain from your product − cost of your product)

[32] https://TheFounderHandbook.org/why-product-and-brand-framing-matters

[33] https://TheFounderHandbook.org/product-premature-optimization

[34] Percentage of requests that have a response time lower than a specific amount. For example, 90% of requests having a response time of 500 milliseconds or less.

[35] https://TheFounderHandbook.org/it-is-not-the-best-product-but-best-execution-that-wins

36 https://TheFounderHandbook.org/race-to-a-category-leader

37 https://TheFounderHandbook.org/what-is-product-market-fit

38 https://TheFounderHandbook.org/how-product-market-fit-feels

39 https://TheFounderHandbook.org/customer-profitability

40 Net MRR churn rate (%) = net MRR churn ($) / MRR from the previous month ($) × 100; Net MRR churn ($) = MRR lost to downgrades and cancellations ($) - new MRR added from existing customers ($). Adjust reporting period in line with your average sales cycle.

41 https://TheFounderHandbook.org/startup-churn-rate

42 https://TheFounderHandbook.org/startup-growth-rate

43 https://TheFounderHandbook.org/company-funding-types

44 https://TheFounderHandbook.org/startup-fundraising-napkin

45 https://TheFounderHandbook.org/why-low-burn-rate-is-important

46 https://TheFounderHandbook.org/rolling-venture-funds

47 https://TheFounderHandbook.org/build-network-effects

48 https://TheFounderHandbook.org/focus-on-building-trust-with-investors-first

49 https://TheFounderHandbook.org/brain-rape

50 https://TheFounderHandbook.org/structure-of-vc-investing

51 https://TheFounderHandbook.org/how-to-find-a-cofounder

52 https://TheFounderHandbook.org/most-startups-fail

53 https://TheFounderHandbook.org/know-what-type-of-sales-you-need-for-your-stage

54 https://TheFounderHandbook.org/build-a-strong-network

55 https://TheFounderHandbook.org/flexible-sales-compensation-structure

56 https://TheFounderHandbook.org/know-the-right-incentives-for-sales

57 https://TheFounderHandbook.org/why-feedback-culture-matters

58 https://TheFounderHandbook.org/why-negative-feedback-rarely-works

59 https://TheFounderHandbook.org/the-alliance-framework

60 https://TheFounderHandbook.org/always-praise-good-work

61 https://TheFounderHandbook.org/to-cry-wolf

62 https://TheFounderHandbook.org/body-language-is-as-important-as-words

63 https://TheFounderHandbook.org/emotions-are-contagious

64 https://TheFounderHandbook.org/what-motivates-type-a-players

65 https://TheFounderHandbook.org/why-enterprise-sales-is-hard

66 https://TheFounderHandbook.org/leading-indicators-of-relationship-failure

67 https://TheFounderHandbook.org/why-mean-people-fail

68 https://TheFounderHandbook.org/diverse-teams-make-better-decisions

Acknowledgements

Special thanks to everyone who helped us make this book happen, and especially to:

- Siobhan's parents, family, nephews and nieces – for making Siobhan happen;
- Andrius's mum and grandparents – for unconditional love, sacrifice and constant support in all shenanigans;
- Entrepreneur First (Alice, Matt and the team), Episode 1 (Ash, Paul, Simon and the team), Business Growth Fund (Henry, Simon and the team) and all AimBrain investors – for believing in us;
- Alesis Novik, David W. Liu, Paul McNabb, Peter Parkanyi, Philip Slingsby and Ruhan Basson – for reviewing our early drafts, suggesting new ideas, guidance, keeping our spirits up and giving us a kick up the butt when needed;
- Simona Petrova – for being a source of happiness, support and unlimited coffee with the brightest smile;
- Juan Aranda – for the patience of many weekends, cups of tea, listening and above all always believing in the best;
- The AimBrain team – for being part of the ride.

Printed in Great Britain
by Amazon